Apple Training Series

iWork '06 with iLife '06

Richard Harrington and RHED Pixel

Apple
Certified

Apple Training Series: iWork '06 with iLife '06
Richard Harrington and RHED Pixel
Copyright © 2006 by Richard Harrington

Published by Peachpit Press. For information on Peachpit Press books, contact:

Peachpit Press
1249 Eighth Street
Berkeley, CA 94710
(510) 524-2178
Fax: (510) 524-2221
http://www.peachpit.com
To report errors, please send a note to errata@peachpit.com
Peachpit Press is a division of Pearson Education

Series Editor: Serena Herr
Managing Editor: Nancy Peterson
Production Coordinator: Laurie Stewart, Happenstance Type-O-Rama
Editor: Judy Ziajka
Copy Editor: Joanne Gosnell
Technical Editor: Victor Gavenda
Media Reviewer: Eric Geoffroy
Compositor: Maureen Forys, Happenstance Type-O-Rama
Indexer: Jack Lewis
Interior Design: Frances Baca
Cover Art Direction: Charlene Charles-Will
Cover Illustration: Kent Oberhu
Cover Production: Chris Gillespie, Happenstance Type-O-Rama
Media Producer: Sara Evans
Media Production: Kevin Bradley, Mark Weiser, Scott Snider, Aronya Waller, Prabha Mohan Mamidipudi, James Ball, Bemnet Goitem, RHED Pixel

ISBN 0-321-44225-3
9 8 7 6 5 4 3 2
Printed and bound in the United States of America

First and always, to Meghan—you complete me in so many ways.
Thanks for your patience and love (especially this time).

To Michael, for keeping it all in perspective and making me smile.

To my family—your guidance and love keeps me on track.

Acknowledgments Much like a successful proposal or presentation, this book was a team project from day one.

A big thanks to Sara Evans and the RHED Pixel team for helping to get this book done. The great projects in this book come from decades of production and design experience.

To the entire production team at Peachpit, thanks for working so hard and being flexible. You create beautiful books, and I hope that this one helps motivate and inspire its audience.

To Patty Montesion and the Apple Education team, thanks for thinking of us for this project. Thanks as well to the iWork team for answering my questions, listening to ideas, and creating such a great suite of programs.

To all of the talented artists, photographers, business owners, and musicians, thanks for helping us make these projects "real-world." Your gifts of images and content have made a big difference.

To our clients, you challenge us to do better, and that led for a search for new tools and techniques. Many of those served as the basis for this book.

To the families of those who worked on this book, thanks for your understanding.

Contents at a Glance

Getting Started xiii

Making Presentations in Keynote

Lesson 1   Creating a Basic Presentation. 3
Lesson 2   Adding Media to Your Presentation 47
Lesson 3   Animating and Viewing Your Presentation 85
Lesson 4   Converting a PowerPoint Presentation 111
Lesson 5   Working with Themes, Graphics, and Hyperlinks. 155
Lesson 6   Publishing and Giving Your Presentation. 203

Publishing with Pages

Lesson 7   Creating a Newsletter 235
Lesson 8   Creating a Marketing Package 271
Lesson 9   Creating a Three-Panel Brochure 309
Lesson 10   Creating a Script, Storyboard, and Presentation 335
Lesson 11   For the Power User (Bonus Lesson) 355

Appendix   Organizing and Refining Your Photos
            (iLife Bonus Lesson) 356

Index. 357

Table of Contents

Getting Started xiii

Making Presentations in Keynote

Lesson 1   Creating a Basic Presentation 3
           Before You Start 4
           Launching Keynote 4
           Choosing a Theme 5
           Selecting a Master Slide 7
           Outlining the Presentation 9
           Working with the Inspector 16
           Formatting Text on a Slide 16
           Customizing a Slide Layout 21
           Copying Styles Between Slides 30
           Cleaning Up the Slides 34
           Adding a Table 36
           Fixing Spelling Errors 43
           Lesson Review 44

Lesson 2   Adding Media to Your Presentation 47
           Accessing Media Files 48
           Working with Still Photos 48
           Adding Photos to Slides 56
           Adding Audio to a Slideshow 64
           Using Video in a Slideshow 69
           Keeping Media with Your Presentation 81
           Lesson Review 82

Lesson 3   Animating and Viewing Your Presentation 85

Creating Builds to Reveal Text 86

Creating a Sequence Build to Reveal a Table 88

Creating Interleaved Builds 90

Watching the Presentation So Far 93

Creating Transitions Between Slides 95

Indexing Your Presentation with Spotlight. 98

Configuring Preferences for Smooth Playback 99

Running Your Presentation 104

Pausing and Resuming a Slideshow. 106

Troubleshooting Your Presentation. 107

Lesson Review 109

Lesson 4   Converting a PowerPoint Presentation 111

Importing a PowerPoint Presentation. 112

Animating the Title Slide 114

Cleaning Up a Chart. 118

Enhancing a Chart 122

Animating a Chart 127

Enhancing a Table 129

Animating a Bar Chart 132

Animating a Pie Chart 135

Changing the Style of a Chart 140

Replacing the Content of a Slide 145

Adding Comments to a Presentation 148

Rehearsing the Presentation. 151

Lesson Review 153

Lesson 5   Working with Themes, Graphics,
and Hyperlinks. 155

Creating a Custom Theme 156

Creating a Background and Formatting Text 161

Creating a Photo Cutout with Photoshop and Keynote 164

Saving and Sharing Themes 174

Applying a Custom Theme. 176

Adding Transparency to Artwork 180

Masking Photos with Shapes 187

Embedding a Web Page 189

Embedding and Formatting QuickTime Movies 191

Adding Hyperlinks and Navigation. 194

Running a Presentation in Kiosk Mode 199

Exporting to CD-ROM. 200

Lesson Review 201

Lesson 6   Publishing and Giving Your Presentation 203

Adding and Printing Speaker Notes 204

Printing Handouts. 206

Exporting to QuickTime 208

Exporting to PowerPoint 211

Exporting to PDF 212

Exporting Images 214

Exporting to Flash. 215

Sending to iDVD. 217

Exporting to HTML 223

Creating a Podcast Using GarageBand 224

Giving Your Presentation with a Laptop. 229

Lesson Review 232

Publishing with Pages

Lesson 7   Creating a Newsletter. 235

Before You Start. 236

Launching Pages 236

Choosing a Template. 237

Working with a Template 239

Replacing Placeholder Text. 241

Editing Image Placeholders 246
Cropping Images Using Masks. 249
Customizing Colors 256
Laying Out More Pages. 259
Inserting a Page into a Layout 263
Completing the Layout. 264
Exporting to PDF 268
Lesson Review 269

Lesson 8   Creating a Marketing Package **271**
Assembling Project Assets. 272
Creating a Poster 273
Creating a Postcard 290
Creating a One-Sheet 304
Lesson Review 307

Lesson 9   Creating a Three-Panel Brochure **309**
Choosing a Template. 310
Customizing the Template 311
Adding Photos. 316
Adding a Background Image 322
Adding Text 324
Lesson Review 333

Lesson 10   Creating a Script, Storyboard,
and Presentation. **335**
Saving a Template for a Video Script. 336
Creating a Storyboard Presentation 340
Publishing a Presentation to .mac 345
Creating a Storyboard Handout 347
Laying Out a Proposal 351
Lesson Review 353

Lesson 11   For the Power User (Bonus Lesson)........... 355
            Exporting Images from Aperture.................. DVD 11-2
            Advanced Text Animation with LiveType........... DVD 11-4
            Creating a Motion Background with LiveType....... DVD 11-9
            Using QuickTime Player to Optimize
              Content for Keynote .... DVD 11-12
            Using Compressor to Optimize Content
              for Keynote................................. DVD 11-15
            Creating Animations with Transparency
              with Motion................................. DVD 11-20
            Creating a PANTONE Color Strip in Photoshop.... DVD 11-24
            Preparing a Layered Photoshop File for
              Import into Keynote or Pages .... DVD 11-27
            Exporting a Chart Animation for Final Cut Pro .... DVD 11-29
            Lesson Review .... DVD 11-32

Appendix   Organizing and Refining Your Photos
            (iLife Bonus Lesson) 356

            Index 357

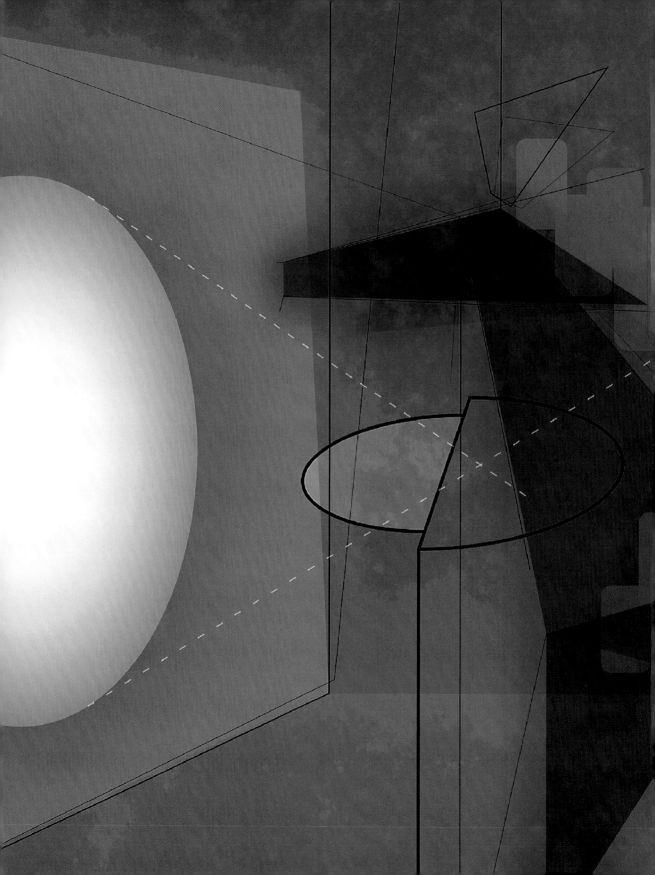

Getting Started

Welcome to the official training course for iWork '06, Apple's software suite for creating publications and presentations. iWork '06 features two powerful applications for creating everything from school newsletters to business presentations. With Pages 2, you can quickly create a wide variety of stunning documents. With Keynote 3, you can produce cinema-quality presentations, storyboards, and more. iWork '06 lets you express yourself with style. Whether you are a student, a business owner, or a creative pro, iWork has the features you need to gather your ideas and publish and present them.

The Methodology

This book emphasizes hands-on training. Each exercise is designed to help you learn the application inside and out. You'll learn how to organize your ideas and then present or publish them with maximum clarity and visual impact. If you are new to iWork, it would be helpful for you to start at the beginning and progress through each lesson in order, since each lesson builds on information learned in previous ones. If you have some experience, you can choose to start with the chapters that address Pages or Keynote directly. This book assumes a basic level of familiarity with the Apple OS X operating system.

Course Structure

Each of the 11 lessons in this book focuses on a different aspect of project creation and distribution using iWork and iLife. Each lesson expands on the basic concepts of the program, giving you the tools to use Pages and Keynote for your own projects.

The lessons in this book are divided into two groups:

▶   Lessons 1–6: Making Presentations in Keynote

▶   Lessons 7–10: Publishing with Pages

You will also find bonus projects for the creative professional in Lesson 11 on the DVD.

System Requirements

Before beginning to use *Apple Training Series: iWork '06 with iLife '06*, you should have a working knowledge of your computer and its operating system. Make sure that you know how to use the mouse and the standard menus and commands and also how to open, save, and close files. If you need to review these techniques, see the printed or online documentation included with your system.

Basic system requirements for iWork '06 are as follows:

▶   Mac OS X version 10.3.9 or 10.4.3 or later

▶   Macintosh computer with a 500MHz or faster PowerPC G4, PowerPC G5, or Intel Core processor

▶   256 MB of RAM (512 MB recommended)

▶   32 MB of video RAM

▶   QuickTime 7.0.3 or later

▶   DVD drive (required for installation)

▶   iLife '06 (recommended)

Basic system requirements for iLife '06 are as follows:

▶   Mac OS X version 10.3.9 or 10.4.3 or later (10.4.4 recommended)

▶   Macintosh computer with a PowerPC G4, PowerPC G5, or Intel Core processor, 733MHz or faster for iDVD

▶   256 MB of RAM (512 MB recommended)

- iTunes 6.0.2 and QuickTime 7.0.4 (included)
- DVD drive (required for installation)
- 10 GB of available disk space
- High-definition video requires a 1GHz G4 or faster processor and 512 MB of RAM
- Burning DVDs requires an Apple SuperDrive or compatible third-party DVD burner

Installing iLife

To install iWork, double-click the iWork installer and follow the instructions that appear.

If you see a message saying that you do not have sufficient privileges to install this software, click the lock icon in the installer window and enter an administrator name and password. The administrators of your computer are listed in the Accounts pane of System Preferences.

Copying the Lesson Files

This book includes an *ATS_iWork_06* DVD-ROM containing all the files you'll need to complete the lessons. Inside the iWork '06 Lessons folder are Lesson subfolders organized by lesson number. Within each numbered Lesson subfolder, you will find projects for each exercise.

When you install these files on your computer, it's important to keep all of the numbered Lesson subfolders together in the main Lessons folder on your hard drive. If you copy the Lessons folder directly from the DVD-ROM to your hard drive, you should not need to reconnect any media files or have problems opening projects.

Installing the Lesson Files

1   Insert the *ATS_iWork_06* DVD-ROM into your computer's DVD-ROM drive.

2   Open the DVD-ROM and drag the iWork '06 Lessons folder from the
     DVD to your computer's desktop.

3   To begin each lesson, launch the specified application (either Keynote or
     Pages). Then follow the instructions in the exercises to open the project
     files for that lesson.

About the Apple Training Series

iWork '06 with iLife '06 is part of the official training series for Apple
iWork applications developed by experts in the field and certified by Apple
Computer. The lessons are designed to let you learn at your own pace.

For those who prefer to learn in an instructor-led setting, Apple also offers
training courses at Apple Authorized Training Centers worldwide. These
courses, which use the Apple Training Series books as their curriculum, are
taught by Apple Certified Trainers and balance concepts and lectures with
hands-on labs and exercises. Apple Authorized Training Centers have been
carefully selected and have met Apple's highest standards in all areas, including facilities, instructors, course delivery, and infrastructure. The goal of the
program is to offer Apple customers, from beginners to the most seasoned
professionals, the highest-quality training experience.

To find an Authorized Training Center near you, go to www.apple.com/
software/pro/training.

Resources

Apple Training Series: iWork '06 with iLife '06 is not intended to be a comprehensive reference manual, nor does it replace the documentation that comes
with the application. For comprehensive information about program features,
refer to these resources:

▶   The Reference Guide. Accessed through the Keynote and Pages Help menus,
     the Reference Guide contains a complete description of all features.

▶   Apple's Web site: www.apple.com.

Making Presentations
in Keynote

1

Lesson Files

Lessons > Lesson 01 > 01PresentationText.txt

Lessons > Lesson 01 > 01Presentation1_Stage2.key

Lessons > Lesson 01 > 01Presentation1_Stage3.key

Lessons > Lesson 01 > 01Presentation1_Stage4.key

Lessons > Lesson 01 > 01Presentation1_Stage5.key

Time

This lesson takes approximately 1 hour to complete.

Goals

Choose a theme

Use master slides

Create an outline to build a presentation

Work with the Inspector window

Work with the Font panel

Check for spelling errors

Lesson **1**

Creating a Basic Presentation

Keynote, included in iWork '06, is Apple's program for creating dynamic presentations. With Keynote, you can build presentations that include text, photos, audio, and video to inform and entertain your audience. Learning how to add and integrate a variety of elements is essential to building a dynamic presentation.

You will start your work in Keynote by creating a basic Keynote presentation. You will first choose a theme to apply to your presentation. Next, you will outline your presentation to create its structure and begin adding text content. Then, using the Inspector and other windows, you will make adjustments to the layout of the text. You'll also learn how to catch spelling errors before you stand at the front of an audience.

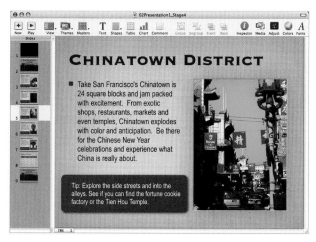

Keynote allows you to create attractive slides by adding your content to well-designed templates.

Before You Start

Before you start this lesson, you need to load the iWork '06 suite onto your hard drive. You also need to copy the lesson files from the DVD in the back of this book to your computer.

The instructions for loading the software and files are in "Getting Started," the introduction to this book. Once those two steps are complete, you can move forward with this lesson.

With iWork '06 and the lesson files loaded onto your hard drive, you are ready to start this lesson.

Launching Keynote

Keynote is the part of iWork '06 that we are working with first. There are three ways to launch Keynote:

▶   Double-click the iWork '06 folder in your Applications folder and then double-click Keynote.

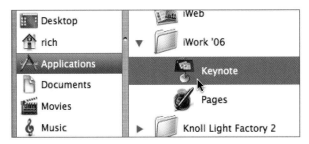

▶   Click the Keynote icon in the Dock once.

► Double-click any Keynote project file.

For this exercise, you'll launch Keynote using the first method.

1 From the Finder, choose File > New Finder Window.

> **NOTE** ► If you haven't copied the Lessons folder of this book to your hard drive, do so at this time.

2 Double-click the Applications folder icon to open the folder.

3 Locate the iWork '06 folder and double-click to open it.

4 Double-click the Keynote application icon to launch the program.

Choosing a Theme

When you first launch Keynote, you are presented with the Theme Chooser window, where you can browse the available themes. A theme is a starting template for your presentation that contains styled backgrounds and slide layouts. Keynote 3 ships with 27 built-in themes, and you can create your own or acquire others from online vendors. Choosing a theme is the first step in creating your Keynote project.

1 If the Theme Chooser window is not visible, choose File > New.

The Theme Chooser window opens.

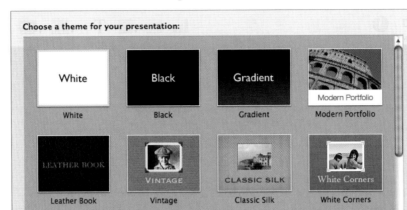

2 Browse the available themes by scrolling through the Theme Chooser window.

A representative thumbnail (generally of a title slide) is shown to assist you. Themes contain multiple slide types to serve special purposes.

3 Click the thumbnail for the Classic Silk theme to select it.

4   From the Slide Size pop-up menu, choose 1024 × 768.

This is the size you'll use for this presentation. The sizes available vary by theme.

NOTE ▶ Some Keynote themes have only two resolutions available: 800 × 600 or 1024 × 768.These are the two most common resolution settings for computer monitors and projects used for presentations. Newer Keynote themes offer three additional sizes. The 1280 × 720 and 1920 × 1080 resolutions match the two most common sizes for HD displays. The other option, 1680 × 1050, is a common resolution setting for Cinema displays.

5   Click Choose to select the theme and create a new document.

6   Choose File > Save. Name your file **Project 1.key** and save it to your local hard drive.

Selecting a Master Slide

Each theme offers a variety of master slides that you can use for your presentation. A master slide is a preset arrangement of text or information that you can select based on your personal preference and your purpose for each slide. If you add photos or a chart to a slide, for instance, you will likely want a different layout than for a slide that contains bullet points of information.

1   Click the Masters button at the top of your document window (on the toolbar) to see a list of master slides.

2   Choose the Title & Bullets master.

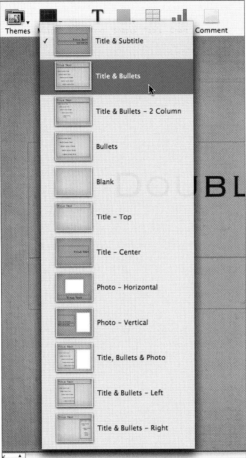

The slide layout changes to the new arrangement. You will use this basic presentation slide layout for your first slide.

TIP Clicking the Masters button lets you choose a new layout. You should examine a theme closely and look at the available master slides. This approach will help you choose a theme for your layout as you can decide based on style and function.

Outlining the Presentation

When building a presentation, many users choose to jump right in and start creating slides. They add text, artwork, and animation one slide at a time. While this approach is valid, many experienced presenters strongly favor creating an outline first.

A presentation is often more coherent when you build it in stages. Think of the process as being similar to building a house. Sure, you could build and finish one room at a time, but most contractors like to start with blueprints, then build a frame, and then move forward from there.

Keynote has a robust outline view, and it is an excellent tool for setting up the content of your presentation. You are going to create a multi-slide presentation using the outline view.

1 In the toolbar, click the View button.

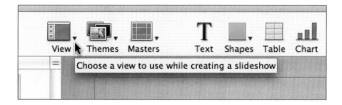

2 Choose Outline view from the list that appears.

As you work with a presentation, you will often change your view to better suit specific tasks.

To make more room for typing, you can expand the slide organizer.

3   Move your cursor over the resize handle at the bottom of the slide organizer.

The cursor changes to a resize cursor.

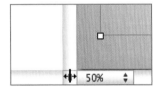

4   Drag to the right to expand the viewable area for your slide organizer.

Creating the First Slide

It's now time to begin building your presentation slides. You'll add some text to your first slide layout. By adding the text in Outline view, you accomplish two things. You have a detailed outline that is easy to modify and share, plus you can quickly build slides with text content.

1   In the Outline column, click to the right of the slide thumbnail with the number 1 next to it.

The area turns light blue, and the insertion point blinks.

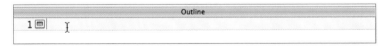

2   Type the following title into the slide:

San Francisco Tourism

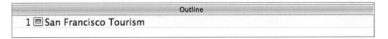

Adding More Slides

For the next slides, you'll use a different master slide. This is because you'll be adding images to the slides in the next lesson. Keynote provides master slides set up for that purpose.

1 Click the New button at the top of the document window to add a new slide.

The number 2 appears next to your new slide.

2 From the Masters list, choose the Title, Bullets & Photo layout.

3 Next to the number 2, type the following title:

Cable Cars

4 Press Return.

A new slide is created. You'll add bullet point information and connect it to slide 2.

5 Press Tab.

The insertion point moves to an indented location underneath the Cable Cars title, and the next text that you type will become a bullet point for this slide.

6 Type the following text in the outline:

Take a ride in one of the oldest cable cars in the nation. San Francisco's cable cars still run today on 8.8 miles of track along three of their original hundred-year-old routes. San Francisco's cable cars are propelled mechanically by a steel cable the cars grip in between one of the slots.

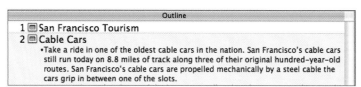

7 Press Return to create a new bullet and then type the following information in the outline:

Tip: For a leisurely ride, avoid the lines at Powell and Market Streets and get on the California line where California Street intersects Market near the Ferry Building.

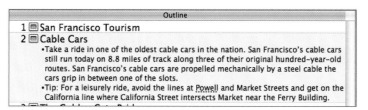

Now add a third slide.

8 Click the New button at the top of the window to add another new slide.

The number 3 appears next to your new slide. The Title, Bullets & Photo layout should still be active since you used it last.

Pasting Text into the Outline

If you already have text typed elsewhere, you can paste it onto your slides instead of typing it. This can speed things up by cutting down on repeated effort.

1   Open the program TextEdit in your Applications folder on your hard drive.

TextEdit

2   Choose File > Open and navigate to the file **PresentationText.txt** in the Lesson 01 folder.

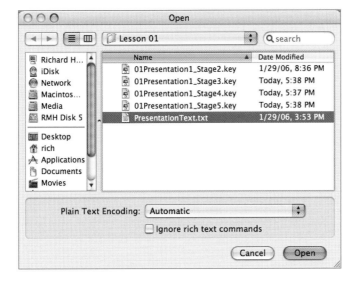

3   Click Open to open the text document.

This document contains the remaining text for your presentation.

TIP ▸ When you save your slide outline in a word processor, save it as a basic text file (.txt). This will prevent the document from containing formatting that can conflict with a theme's look.

You need to put the text on your clipboard to use it.

4 Choose Edit > Select All to select all of the text in the document; then choose Edit > Copy to copy the text to the clipboard.

5 Return to Keynote.

>  A quick way to switch between open applications is to press Command-Tab. This will display a bar with all open applications. Click the Keynote icon to switch to it.

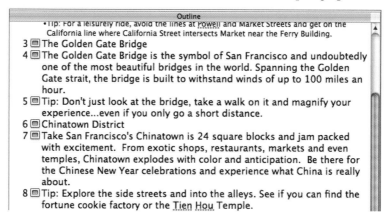

6 Click the empty area next to slide 3. Then choose Edit > Paste.

The text is added, and a new slide is created for each paragraph of text.

> **Outline**
>
> •Tip: For a leisurely ride, avoid the lines at Powell and Market Streets and get on the California line where California Street intersects Market near the Ferry Building.
> 3 ▢ The Golden Gate Bridge
> 4 ▢ The Golden Gate Bridge is the symbol of San Francisco and undoubtedly one of the most beautiful bridges in the world. Spanning the Golden Gate strait, the bridge is built to withstand winds of up to 100 miles an hour.
> 5 ▢ Tip: Don't just look at the bridge, take a walk on it and magnify your experience...even if you only go a short distance.
> 6 ▢ Chinatown District
> 7 ▢ Take San Francisco's Chinatown is 24 square blocks and jam packed with excitement. From exotic shops, restaurants, markets and even temples, Chinatown explodes with color and anticipation. Be there for the Chinese New Year celebrations and experience what China is really about.
> 8 ▢ Tip: Explore the side streets and into the alleys. See if you can find the fortune cookie factory or the Tien Hou Temple.

You need to rearrange the text blocks so the slide title and two bullets appear on each page.

NOTE ▶ Some of the text contains spelling errors. This is on purpose, and you'll fix it later in the lesson.

7 Click slide 4 and press the Tab key to indent the text.

The block should indent and now be located on slide 3. Old slide 5 (the tip) now becomes slide 4.

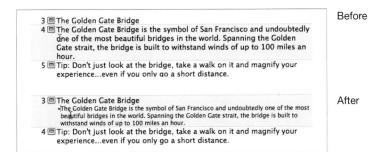

Before

After

Repeat this indenting action for the next bullet.

8   Click slide 4 and press the Tab key to indent the text.

That block should also indent and become a bullet on slide 3.

9   Format the rest of your slides so each has a title and two bullets of information (the last slide has just a title).

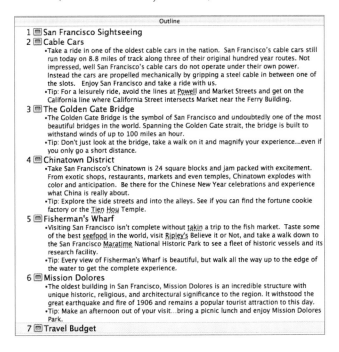

10   When you're done, check your work by looking at **01Presentation1_ Stage2.key**.

Working with the Inspector

The Inspector window is extremely important in Keynote. It contains inspectors with most of the controls you will use to format, stylize, and animate your presentation. It is a good idea to leave the Inspector window open (if it's closed, click the Inspector button on the toolbar). To switch between inspectors for particular tasks, click the appropriate button in the top bar.

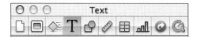

The Inspector window gives you access to these inspectors:

▶ **Document:** Set your slideshow properties as well as Spotlight comments.

▶ **Slide:** Create transitions between slides and control slide appearance.

▶ **Build:** Animate the text and other elements on your slide to reveal information.

▶ **Text:** Format the layout of text and bullets on the canvas.

▶ **Graphic:** Control the properties and appearance of graphics.

▶ **Metrics:** Size and position elements.

▶ **Table:** Create and format tables to hold data.

▶ **Chart:** Control the properties of charts and graphs.

▶ **Hyperlink:** Add Web links, links to slides, and Web pages to your presentation.

▶ **QuickTime:** Control the properties of QuickTime files in your document.

You will use the Text, Graphic, and Table Inspectors as you begin your presentation project. You will be working with all of the inspectors in the course of this book.

Formatting Text on a Slide

Now that you have completed your outline, you can begin to format your slides. Before you focus on spicing up your slides with photos and animation, you'll want to format the text to achieve a clean and professional layout. Good presentations start with good text.

1   Choose View > Navigator.

The navigator view is good for browsing and modifying your presentation. It displays two columns. The left column contains a thumbnail for each slide, and the right column shows the slide canvas, which is an editable version of the slide.

2   Click the thumbnail for slide 1 to select it.

You are going to change the first slide to accommodate a photo and title.

3 Click the Masters button and choose Title – Center.

The background color changes, as does the layout of the text.

4 Triple-click the slide's title in the slide canvas to select it.

The text is highlighted in light blue, indicating that it is active and ready for modification.

5 Click the Fonts button in the toolbar to open the Font panel.

6   In the Family list, ensure that the font Copperplate is selected, and in the Typeface list, click Bold to change the style of the title font.

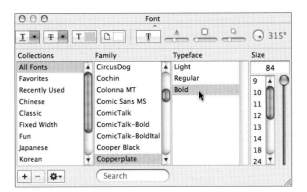

7   In the Font panel, change the font size to 96 points.

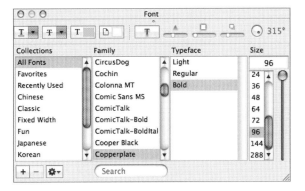

8   Click in the slide canvas area below the text to deselect the text.

9   Click the title text block to select it.

10   Click the Text Inspector button to switch to the Text Inspector.

The Text Inspector allows you to modify text alignment, spacing, and color.

11   Click the Text button to view text properties (this button should be high-lighted by default). Click the Center text alignment button to center your text within the text block.

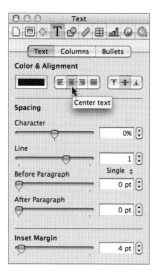

12   In the slide canvas, drag the text block slowly to the left and toward the top of the slide. Drag until the object snaps to the yellow pop-up alignment guides.

The title is now centered horizontally on the page. Pop-up alignment guides are useful for visually positioning elements on a slide with precise alignment.

Customizing a Slide Layout

You have created a simple title slide layout. Now it is time to explore more complex formatting of text. You'll want to be able to format text for readability as well as design.

Modifying the Title

1   Click slide 2 in the Slides list.

2   Triple-click the words Cable Cars in the slide canvas to select them.

3   Press Command-B to make the font in the slide's title bold.

NOTE ▶ This shortcut works only if the font chosen has a bold version available.

Modifying the Bullet Points

1   Click the bullet area of the slide canvas to select the bulleted text block, and then click again within one of the words in the text block to place the insertion point in the text.

2   Choose Edit > Select All to select all of the text in the text block

3   Click the Fonts button to activate the Font panel if it not already visible.

4   In the Family list, click the font Arial Narrow, and in the Typeface list, click Regular.

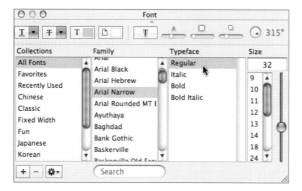

The font for the bullet points changes, and more words fit on the page. Some of the words are cut off, however, so you'll have to make the text smaller.

5   Drag the Size slider downward in the Font panel until all of the words fit in the text block. A point size of 30 or 31 should work.

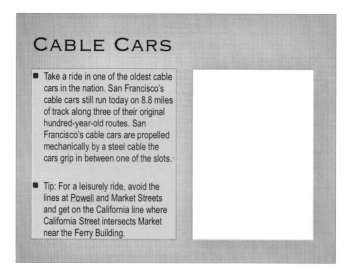

Dragging the slider down reduces the point size of the text. You can also change size by typing an exact number in the Size field or by choosing a preset from the Size preset list.

Adding a Shape to Hold Text

You can place text inside a variety of shapes on your slide. Putting text inside a shape is a great way to make it stand out. Let's format the tip text in the slides so it looks different from the bullet point text.

1   Choose Insert > Shape > Rounded Rectangle.

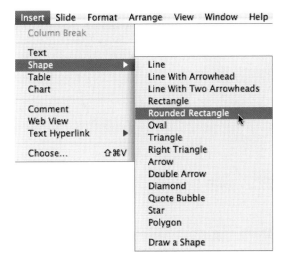

The rectangle is added to the center of the slide, in colors based upon the theme you have chosen. These colors can be easily changed.

2   Switch to the Graphic Inspector.

The Graphic Inspector allows you to modify the fill and stroke of an object as well as the opacity and drop shadow properties.

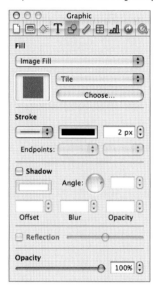

3   Click the Fill pop-up menu and change the fill to Color Fill.

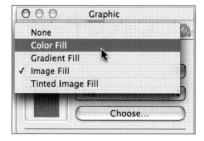

4   Click the color well to open the Colors window.

5   Click the magnifying glass icon to sample colors from your image.

You can select colors from any object in your canvas to colorize text or fill a shape.

6   Click the reddish-brown text bullet to sample that color for the fill.

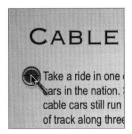

The sample color is loaded into the large strip of color next to the magnifying glass and into the Fill color well in the Graphic Inspector.

7   Drag the color from the Colors window into the Stroke color well to change it to brown.

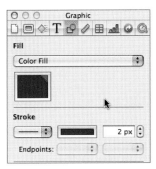

Placing Text Inside a Shape

One benefit of adding shapes is that they can serve as containers for text. This allows you to place text in a styled shape.

1   Triple-click the tip text at the bottom of the slide to select it.

2   Choose Edit > Cut to place the text on your clipboard.

3   Press Delete to remove the second bullet from the layout.

The text block is no longer aligned at the top of the text box. This is because the default alignment for the master slide is set to centered.

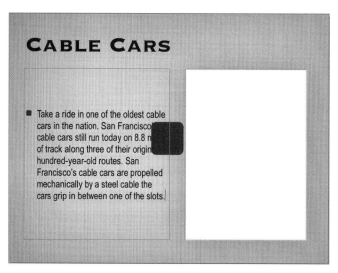

4 Switch to the Text Inspector and click the Align text to top of table cell, text box, or shape button.

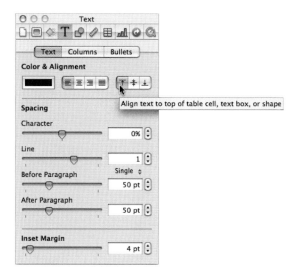

The text is now aligned at the top of the text block.

5 Double-click the rounded rectangle to place the text cursor inside.

6 Choose Edit > Paste to paste the text from your clipboard.

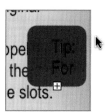

The text is added inside the shape. However, much of it is cut off, and the black text on brown background is hard to read.

NOTE ▸ The plus symbol at the bottom of the shape indicates that there are more characters inside the shape. The block must be made larger or the text must be made smaller, or both, so the text can be seen.

7   Press Command-A to select all of the text.

8   In the Colors window, click a white swatch from the bottom of the window.

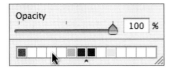

9   Drag the white swatch onto the text to change the text color to white.

10 In the Text Inspector, click the Bullets button.

11 Change the following settings:

▶ Set Indent Level to 1.

▶ Set Bullets & Numbering to No Bullets.

▶ Set Text Indent to 0 px.

12 Click outside the text block to deselect it.

13 Click the edge of the rounded rectangle. Drag the edges of the shape to make the shape larger. Resize the block so all of the text is readable.

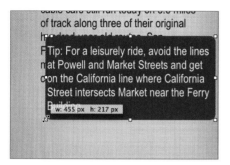

14 Click the Graphic Inspector to activate it.

15 Select the Shadow check box to turn on a drop shadow for the rounded rectangle.

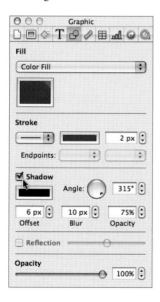

The default Shadow settings are fine for this design.

16 Drag and position the rounded rectangle below your bulleted text block.

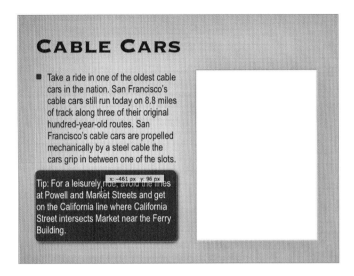

You can use alignment guides to help you position the box accurately.

Copying Styles Between Slides

Once a slide is formatted, you can copy elements and styles from one slide and paste them onto another. This approach can help you maintain consistency in your presentation. In this project, slides 3 to 6 should match slide 2.

Styling the Titles

Using a consistent format for text blocks is important. It can improve readability as well as the appearance of your presentation.

1 In Navigator view, select slide 2.

2 In the slide canvas, triple-click the words Cable Cars to select this text.

3   Choose Format > Copy Style.

This command loads the format of the text, including its font, typeface, color, and point size, onto your clipboard.

4   Switch to slide 3 in the slide organizer.

5   In the slide canvas, triple-click the words The Golden Gate Bridge to select them.

6   Choose Format > Paste Style.

The title changes to match the style of slide 2. However, the last word is cut off.

NOTE ▶ The plus symbol at the bottom of a text block indicates that the block contains text that is not visible. You must reduce the point size or enlarge the text block, or both, so that all characters fit. When the text block has been modified so that all characters are displayed, the plus sign disappears.

7 Reduce the size of the title to 72 points. You can do this using the Font panel.

Styling the Bullets

The look of the bullets on one page can also be applied to other pages. Doing so is important for consistency in your presentation.

1 Select slide 2 in the slide organizer.

2 In the slide canvas, click once within the bullet text area to select the text block; then click again in the text to place the insertion point within the bullet point text.

> ■ Take a ride in one of the oldest cable cars in the nation. San Francisco's cable cars still run today on 8.8 miles of track along three of their original hundred-year-old routes. San Francisco's cable cars are propelled mechanically by a steel cable the cars grip in between one of the slots.

3 Choose Format > Copy Style.

4 Switch to slide 3 in the slide organizer.

5   Double-click the bullet copy to edit it; then choose Edit > Select All.

6   Choose Format > Paste Style.

Both bullets now share the same style.

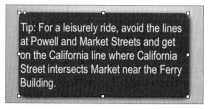

Adding the Rounded Rectangle

1   Select slide 2 in the slide organizer.

2   Click the rounded rectangle shape to select it.

3   Choose Edit > Copy.

4   Switch to slide 3 in the slide organizer.

5   Choose Edit > Paste to add a copy of the rounded rectangle to slide 3.

6   Select the bullet text block (the tip you just pasted will be partially obscuring it). Bring it to the front by choosing Arrange > Bring to Front.

7   Select the text of the second bullet by triple-clicking the second bullet.

8   Choose Edit > Cut to remove the text from your slide and place it on the clipboard; then press Delete to remove the second bullet. Send the text block to the back by choosing Arrange > Send to Back.

9   Double-click inside of the rounded rectangle to select all of the text.

You want to replace the text with the contents of your clipboard, but you also want to preserve the existing formatting.

10   Choose Edit > Paste and Match Style.

11   Resize the rounded rectangle as needed so the text fits and is readable.

Tip: Don't just look at the bridge, take a walk on it and magnify your experience... even if you only go a short distance.

Cleaning Up the Slides

Even though your text is entered, your slides can benefit from a little touchup to the formatting. It is important to polish your layout to create a professional-looking presentation. Select the bulleted text to make it active before you get started.

1   Switch to the Text Inspector and click the Text button; then click the "Align text to top of table cell, text box, or shape" button to fix the text block.

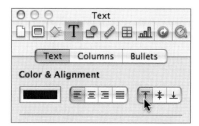

2 Drag the bottom edge of the text block toward the top to make the box smaller.

3 Adjust the point size of all elements so they are readable. Do not make text too large or text will be clipped (if you see the plus symbol, your text is too large).

4 Adjust the size of the bullet to taste.

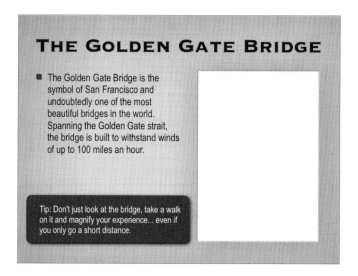

You should now have cleaned up slides 2 and 3. If you like, you can clean up all of your slides, or you can open the file **01Presentation1_Stage3.key** and use it for the remainder of this lesson.

Adding a Table

Slide 7 contains information on the cost of travel and lodging. This slide needs to be updated to present the information cleanly. You can use a table to do this task quite nicely.

1   Select slide 7 in the slide organizer.

You need a different slide layout to better accommodate a table.

2 Click the Masters button in the toolbar and choose Title – Top.

3 Select the text in the title and press Command-B to make it bold.

4 Choose Insert > Table to add a table to the slide or click the Table button in the toolbar.

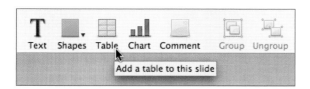

Keynote automatically switches to the Table Inspector and adds a 3 by 3 table to your slide.

5 Select the Header Row check box.

A new row is added to the top of the table.

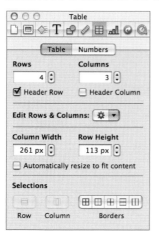

6 In the Columns field, enter *4*.

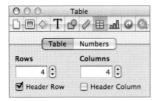

7 Resize the table by dragging the handles at the corners or in the center of each edge. Make it fill the bottom area of the slide.

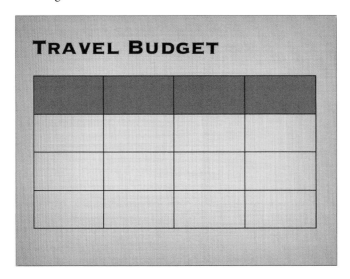

Use alignment guides to check whether the table is centered horizontally.

Filling the Table Header Row

A table header row identifies the contents of a table, helping viewers understand the information they are seeing.

1 Enter the following text in the first four cells at the top of the table.

Departure City   Airfare   Hotel   Total

The first cell wraps the text in an unusual way because the text is too large to fit.

TRAVEL BUDGET			
DEPARTUR E CITY	AIRFARE	HOTEL	TOTAL

2 Make sure the table is selected; then click within the first cell of the table header row (Departure City) to select that cell.

The cell should have a gold border.

3 Hold down the Shift key and click the last cell of the table header row (Total).

All four cells are now selected and outlined in gold.

DEPARTUR E CITY	AIRFARE	HOTEL	TOTAL

4 Open the Font panel and modify the text to fit. Choose a point size of 36 and a bold typeface.

DEPARTURE CITY	AIRFARE	HOTEL	TOTAL

Filling the Table Cells

Now that the table is properly set up, we can populate it. Adding data to each cell will communicate information to the viewer. Additionally, we can use calculations to perform mathematical functions on the contents of the table.

1   Enter the information shown here in your table.

TRAVEL BUDGET			
DEPARTURE CITY	AIRFARE	HOTEL	TOTAL
CHICAGO	$400	$600	
SEATTLE	$250	$600	
NEW YORK	$575	$600	

iWork '06 can perform calculations within tables. Here, you can let the software determine the total costs based on the values entered in the Airfare and Hotel fields. This feature is useful if your have a lot of numbers or values that frequently change.

2   Click the table to select it; then click the header for the fourth column (the word *Total*).

NOTE ▶ Be sure to click once each time! Otherwise, you'll modify the contents of the cell.

3   Type an equals sign (=).

The Formula Editor opens. Along the top and left sides of the table, you can now see the letters and numbers that identify the columns and rows of the table grid. You are going to enter a formula so that Keynote will calculate the total of airfare and hotel costs for you automatically.

4   Click the column header cell for column B (Airfare) and then click the column header cell for column C (Hotel).

The Formula Editor displays =B+C. It will add the numbers in columns B and C and place the result in column D.

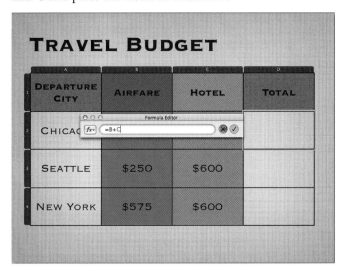

5   Press Return to apply the formula.

Keynote correctly adds the two numbers for you. The formatting, however, needs to be adjusted.

6   Select the three text cells in column D.

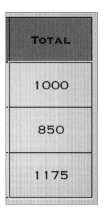

7   In the Table Inspector, click the Numbers button to see the formatting options.

8   Select the Number Format check box and set the following options:

▶   Set Prefix to $.

▶   Set Separator to 1,000.

▶   Set Decimals to 0.

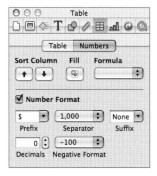

You can check your work by opening the file **01Presentation1_Stage4.key**.

Fixing Spelling Errors

Spelling errors are common when creating any sort of text. Regardless of where errors came from, you'll want to catch them in your presentation before it goes in front of an audience.

The text that you copied has a few spelling errors. They were placed there on purpose for this exercise.

1   Click slide 5 in the slide organizer. Look closely at the text block; words underlined in red are misspelled.

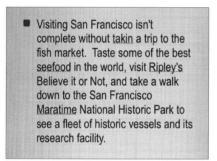

2   Choose Edit > Spelling > Spelling.

The Spelling window opens. It allows you to browse spelling errors and suggests replacement words.

3   The first spelling error on slide 5 is "takin." Select "taking" from the Guess list and click Correct.

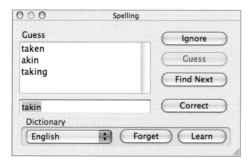

4 The next spelling error is "seefood." Select "seafood" from the Guess list and click Correct.

5 The next highlighted word is "Ripley's." This word is spelled correctly. Click the Ignore button.

6 The next spelling error is "Maratime." Select "Maritime" from the Guess list and click Correct.

When Keynote finishes checking the active slide, it goes to the next slide in the document that it thinks contains errors.

7 There are no additional errors in this document, so you can close the Spelling window.

8 You can check your work by comparing it to **01Presentation1_ Stage5.key.**

Lesson Review

1. How do you choose a theme?
2. Where are master slides located?
3. How should text be formatted for pasting into the slide organizer when in outline view?
4. How do you change the functionality of the Inspector window?
5. How do you activate the Spelling window?

Answers

1. Themes can be chosen from the Theme Chooser window. This window opens automatically when you create a new document or when you choose File > Choose Theme.

2. You can access master slides by clicking the Masters button in the toolbar. The available master slides will be shown in the list that appears.

3. Text that you want to copy from your word processor into Keynote should be saved as a plain text file (.txt).

4. The inspectors serve many purposes (from graphic editing to object and text alignment). At the top of the Inspector window is a row of buttons that you can use to switch from one inspector to another.

5. Choose Edit > Spelling > Spelling to open the Spelling window.

2

Lesson Files

Lessons > Lesson 02 > 02Presentation1_Stage1.key

Lessons > Lesson 02 > GarageBand > San Francisco Music Bed.band

Lessons > Lesson 02 > iMovie Project > SF Tourism.iMovieProject, SF Tourism Finished.iMovieProject

Lessons > Lesson 02 > iPhoto Images

Time

This lesson takes approximately 1 hour to complete.

Goals

Understand supported media types

Create an album in iPhoto

Export a GarageBand song

Create an MP3 file in iTunes

Export a video file from iMovie

Optimize a video for playback in Keynote

Add photos, audio, and video from the Media Browser window

Lesson 2

Adding Media to Your Presentation

Although text is often the most important part of a presentation, it is the supporting media that can truly make a presentation special. Keynote supports a wide variety of media formats, including formats for graphics, sound, and movies. The heart of this graphic support is QuickTime, the versatile media player on your Mac. In fact, if you can open a file in QuickTime, you can use it in Keynote. This great flexibility makes it easy for you to design enhanced presentations.

While Keynote supports several formats, some work better than others. Also, by optimizing your files, you can make your presentation files smaller, allowing smoother playback and easier portability. Fortunately, preparing your files is easy—you have all the tools you need on your Mac by default. By harnessing the friendly, flexible iLife applications, you can get the job done.

Keynote allows you to browse your iLife media libraries.

Accessing Media Files

The method for accessing your media files depends on where you store them. If you store files in systemwide default locations (such as your iPhoto or iTunes library or the Movies folder), you can use the Media Browser feature in Keynote to access them. Alternatively, you can use the Insert > Choose command to access files that you've stored elsewhere on your hard drive.

Both methods work well, and we'll use them both throughout these lessons. For now, you'll work from iLife's default locations. For these exercises, you'll be using iLife '06. If you do not have this version, you will find the intermediate files in the Lessons folder so you can skip ahead.

Working with Still Photos

One way to organize images for use in Keynote is to use iPhoto. This flexible application allows you to process, size, and organize your photos. As an added benefit, the changes you make to images in iPhoto are applied nondestructively, which means that you can change your mind and restore the original image (even after you close the program).

Adding Photos to iPhoto

If you have images that you want use in your presentation, you can add them to iPhoto, so you can more easily manage and adjust them. While most users add photos to iPhoto by transferring them from a digital camera, there are other ways. Here, you'll add six images to iPhoto.

1   Open the **iPhoto Images** folder in the Lesson 02 folder.

The folder contains six photos.

2   Select the six photos and drag them onto the iPhoto icon in your Dock.

3   Release the mouse button to complete the import.

iPhoto opens and becomes the active application.

When the spinning progress circle stops, the photos are in your iPhoto library.

Creating an Album in iPhoto

An iPhoto album is an excellent means of organizing your photos for use in Keynote. Albums are also easy to create.

1 Click the Last Roll icon to see the last photos added to your library.

This icon lets you isolate the most recent photos for quick access.

2 Choose Edit > Select All to select all of the photos imported in the last roll.

3 Drag the photos into an empty area of the Source pane and release the mouse button when the plus symbol appears.

If you have a lot of albums, it may be difficult to find an empty area. If so, simply choose File > New Album from Selection.

A new album called Untitled Album is created. The name is highlighted and ready to be modified.

4 Double-click and name the album *SF Travel Photos* and press Return.

iPhoto albums will show up in Keynote's Media Browser.

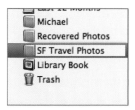

Enhancing Photos with iPhoto

In a perfect world, photos would never need touch-up. This, however, is not the case. Most images—including those you're including in your Keynote presentation—benefit from a little digital attention. While professionals will often turn to applications like Aperture or Adobe Photoshop, several common image problems such as exposure and color balance can be tackled within iPhoto.

1 Select the photo of the cable car in the SF Travel Photos library.

2   Click the Edit button at the bottom of the iPhoto window.

iPhoto switches into Edit mode. This mode allows you to adjust the image as well as enhance or crop it.

3   Click the Enhance button to automatically adjust the color and contrast of the photo.

4   At the top of the window, click the thumbnail for the China Town image.

5 Enhance the China Town image in the library using the same technique as before. Then click the Fisherman's Wharf image in the thumbnail list.

The third photo (of Fisherman's Wharf) is a bit dark and improperly color balanced. The whites in the image are not a clean white; in fact, they have a bit of a color cast to them.

6   Click the Enhance button to help neutralize the blue cast to the image.

7   Click the Adjust button to open the Adjust panel.

Adjust

8   Adjust the Saturation, Temperature, and Exposure sliders. Notice how your image changes as you drag the sliders. Use values close to these.

▶   Saturation: 70

▶   Temperature: 7.8

▶   Exposure: 15.5

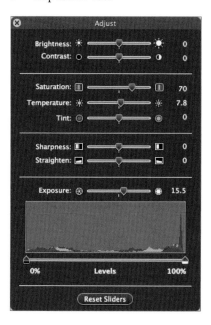

The image should be better exposed and color balanced.

9   Adjust the remaining three images to taste with the Enhance button or the Adjust pane.

10 When you're finished adjusting the images, quit iPhoto.

Adding Photos to Slides

Your photos are now ready to be added to the travel presentation you have been building. The theme we are using contains photo cutouts. Photo cutouts are automatically included in your presentation when you choose slide masters with a photo in them. You can include an image that will appear through the cutout window.

1 Open the file **02Presentation1_Stage1.key** in the Lesson 02 folder.

2   Open the Media Browser by clicking the Media button at the top of your
document window.

3   Choose iPhoto from the Media Browser pop-up menu and click the SF
Travel Photos album.

4   Click slide 2 in the slide organizer.

The Cable Car slide is now selected.

5 Drag the photo **phot_cable_car.jpg** to the cutout window in the slide canvas.

6 Resize the image within the cutout by dragging a corner selection handle (click the corner of the image). Position the photo within the cutout window by dragging the image to adjust its position to taste.

Any portion of the image that extends beyond the cutout window will be hidden when you present your Keynote presentation.

7 From the Media Browser, add the photo **golden_gate_dusk.jpg** to slide 3. Size the image and position it within the cutout window.

8 Add the image **phot_china_town.jpg** to slide 4.

The image is very large, and you won't be able to see the corner handles that let you resize the image.

9 Open the Inspector window and click the Metrics Inspector button. Set the height to 600 px (so the image fits on the slide) and position the image within the photo cutout.

10 Add the image **phot_fishermans_wharf.jpg** to slide 5. Size and position the image using the same techniques as for the previous slide.

Straightening a Photo

The photo that we want to add to our sixth slide needs a little extra fixing.

1 Select slide 6: Mission Dolores.

2 Add the image **phot_mission_dolores.jpg** to the slide.

3 In the Metrics Inspector, set the image height to 650 px to scale the image down.

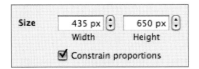

The photo is crooked and needs to be straightened.

4 Choose View > Show Rulers to display the rulers.

5 Drag a guide from the ruler toward the bottom of the photo. Drag it near the edge of the sidewalk.

6 Select the image in the slide canvas by clicking it.

7 Select the Metrics Inspector to access the image properties. Set the angle of the image to 0.9°.

Determining the right number is a matter of trial and error. You can use alignment guides to assist you.

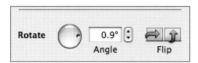

The image is now level. While it's a minor adjustment, it is an important one.

Masking a Photo

Often a photo will not be shaped right for your slide. By masking an image, you can change its shape by hiding parts of it. Masking can help improve the overall layout of the slide.

1 Select slide 1 in the slide organizer.

2 Drag the photo ggate_bay_day.jpg from the Media Browser onto the canvas of slide 1.

3 In the Metrics Inspector, set the width to 1024 px so the image fits on the slide.

4   Drag the photo to reposition it on the slide. Use the alignment guides to center the image horizontally, and line up the bottom of the image with the bottom of the slide.

5   Choose Format > Mask.

Keynote adds a mask to the image that can be resized or repositioned.

6   Drag the corners of the mask so the left and right edges extend beyond the border of the slide. Drag the top and bottom edges to approximately match the image shown here.

7   Press Return to apply the mask.

You can check your progress against the file **02Presentation1_Stage2.key**.

Adding Audio to a Slideshow

Keynote presentations support an audio bed—music or narration that can play underneath your slideshow. This can be used to add narration to individual slides if you are preparing a kiosk or self-running presentation. You also can add music to your presentation so it plays throughout the slideshow.

NOTE ▶ Some audio files are protected under copyright law. You may not have the rights to use an audio file for a presentation. Additionally, if you want to use audio purchased from the iTunes Music Store, the playback machine must be authorized for the files.

TIP ▶ Keynote accepts any QuickTime file type, including MP3, AIFF, and AAC.

Exporting a GarageBand Song

GarageBand is a music composition program that is included with iLife. It allows users of various music abilities to create custom audio. The program is very versatile as it allows you to combine live audio recordings, recordings of digitally synthesized or sampled material input via MIDI, and prerecorded loops.

Let's use a custom song that was created for this project. This audio file will serve as background music for our presentation.

1   Open the **GarageBand** folder in the Lesson 02 folder.

2   Double-click the file **San Francisco Music Bed.band** to open the song and launch GarageBand.

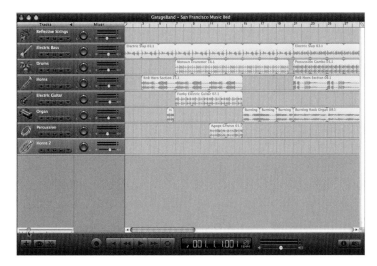

This song was created by RHED Pixel staff member Scott Snider using GarageBand. Feel free to use this song as is or modify it to your liking.

3   In the transport controls at the bottom of the GarageBand window, click the Go to Beginning button.

This moves the playhead to the beginning of the song.

4   Click the Play button to play the song.

If you'd like to adjust the mix or add to the song, feel free. When you're satisfied with the song, you're ready to export it.

5   Choose Share > Send Song to iTunes.

6   The iTunes application starts, and the song is added to your iTunes library and included in a playlist that is named after the machine owner (that is, *Your Name*'s Playlist). The file is a CD-quality AIFF file, which can be used as is—or it can be optimized for Keynote playback, which you'll do next.

Creating an AAC File in iTunes

Once the song is added to your iTunes library, it needs to be optimized. Optimizing the file will ensure that the file plays back smoothly during your presentation.

1   In iTunes, choose iTunes > Preferences to access your user settings.

2   Click the Advanced button; then click Importing.

3   Choose AAC Encoder.

This setting will provide the smallest file size and smoothest playback in your Keynote presentation.

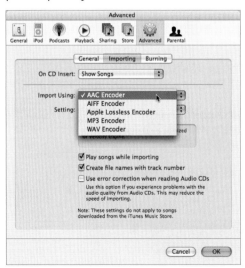

4 Click OK to apply the change to your settings.

5 In the playlist, select the song San Francisco Music Bed.

6 Choose Advanced > Convert Selection to AAC.

The song is converted to AAC format. You can delete the AIFF file since you no longer need it here. When sending a file, GarageBand exports only to uncompressed formats, and you can return to the original project file in GarageBand if you need it in the future.

7 Choose your library in the source list; then in the Search field enter *San Francisco*.

iTunes quickly sifts your library and shows you all songs with the words "San Francisco" in the title.

8 Select the AIFF file and press Delete to remove it from your iTunes library.

The conversion is complete.

9 Choose iTunes > Quit to quit iTunes.

Adding a Music Bed to Your Slideshow

Now that the audio file is prepared, it can be added to your presentation.

1 Press Command-Tab to switch back to Keynote.

This key combination cycles through your open applications.

2   Open the Media Browser.

3   Click the iTunes icon and then type *san francisco* in the search field.

4   In the Inspector window, click the Document button; then click Document.

5   Drag the **San Francisco Music Bed** audio file from the Media Browser into the Audio well.

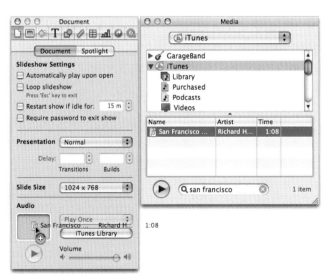

6   In the Document Inspector, choose Loop from the Audio pop-up menu.

The audio file will play continuously during the presentation. If needed, you can adjust the volume of the song.

You can check your project against the file **02Presentation1_Stage3.key**.

Using Video in a Slideshow

Keynote presentations support video elements. These can be used to enhance slide backgrounds or deliver important information. For the presentation we're working on here, we're going to add a video that shows some of the major tourist sites of San Francisco. To ensure that video plays back smoothly, it's a good idea to optimize the files. Files that have been optimized for CD-ROM or Internet delivery will play back well in most presentations. For a thorough discussion of advanced video formats see Chapter 11, "For the Power User."

Preparing a Video in iMovie HD

If you need to edit video clips together into a finished movie, Apple offers you several options including Final Cut Pro, Final Cut Express, and iMovie HD. Each offers different benefits, and all handle video editing tasks well. iMovie HD is an excellent entry into video editing and is well suited for consumer or basic editing tasks. Using iMovie HD, we can prepare a finished clip to introduce our slideshow.

> **NOTE** ▶ If you don't want to edit the video, you can open the file **SF Tourism Finished.iMovieProject** and then skip ahead to the section "Optimizing a Video for Playback." If you don't have access to iMovie HD, you can skip ahead to "Adding Video to a Slide" and use the file **SF Tourism Finished.mov**.

1   Open the **iMovie Project** folder in the Lesson 02 folder.

2   Double-click the file **SF Tourism.iMovieProject** to open it.

iMovie HD launches.

TIP   Be sure to copy the project files to your local hard drive for smooth playback of video files.

3   In this project, you have eight clips to work with. Click the thumbnail showing the Golden Gate bridge to load the clip into the iMovie monitor.

4   Drag the playhead in the scrubber bar below the iMovie monitor to position the shot where you'd like to begin.

5   Place the pointer just below the playhead and drag to the right to choose the footage you want to keep. The crop markers move to the points where you begin and end your drag. Keep about 15 seconds of the shot.

The gold portion of the scrubber bar identifies the footage you've selected.

6   Choose Edit > Crop to keep the selected video and remove the rest.

7   On your own, crop the rest of the movies to shorten them to about 6 to 15 seconds each.

Adding Clips to Your Movie

Once you've trimmed your clips, you can add them to the Timeline. You can arrange them and then add transitions. When you're movie is completed, you can export it for use in Keynote.

1   Click the Clip Viewer button below the iMovie monitor.

2   In the Clips pane, select the Golden Gate clip and drag it to the clip viewer.

3   Repeat step 2 for the other seven clips you want to add to your movie.

4   Drag clips in the clip viewer to rearrange them into the order you want. You will use this montage to introduce your presentation.

5   Choose File > Save Project to save your movie project.

6   Click the Editing button to access the edit controls.

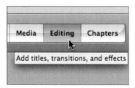

7   Click the Transitions button to access iMovie's transitions.

You're going to add some transitions to make the movement from one slide to the next less jarring.

8   Click the Fade In transition and set the speed to 2:00.

The first video clip will fade in from black.

9   Drag the Fade In transition before the first clip in the Timeline.

10   Choose the Circle Opening transition and drag it between the first and second clips.

This transition will create a circular wipe between clips, to add interest to your presentation.

11 Repeat the Circle Opening transition between the remaining clips.

The red bar indicates that the transition is being processed (or rendered).

12 Click the Timeline viewer button to change your Timeline to a linear view.

This view makes it easier to see how long your sequence is running.

13 Click Play to watch your video sequence.

14 Choose File > Save to save your project.

Optimizing a Video for Playback

The video needs to be exported from iMovie HD and optimized for playback in Keynote.

1 Choose Share > QuickTime to create a movie file.

2   From the "Compress movie for" menu, choose Expert Settings.

3   Click Share.

A new window opens allowing you to customize your movie's compression and playback settings.

4   From the Export menu, choose Movie to QuickTime Movie.

5   Click the Options button to customize the export.

6   Click the Settings button and use the following settings (these settings will give you a good balance between quality and reasonable file size):

▶   Compression Type: H.264

▶   Frame Rate: 15 fps (cutting the frame rate in half reduces the file size by 50 percent)

▶ Data Rate: Automatic

▶ Compressor: Medium

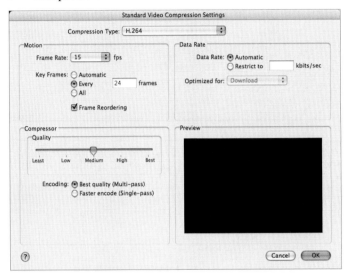

7 Click OK.

8 Click the Size button to set the movie size.

> **NOTE** ▶ Video files often have nonsquare pixels, which are optimized for a television screen. You must convert the video for playback in Keynote. In the next step, you'll change the size of the video in order to convert the pixels from nonsquare to square.

9 Select Use custom size. Enter a width of 640 and a height of 480; then click OK.

10 Click OK again.

11 Navigate to the Movies folder in your User folder and save the movie as *SF Tourism.mov*.

12 Save your project and quit the iMovie.

Adding Video to a Slide

Placing video on a slide is similar to adding a photo. You just navigate to the file and drag the video onto a slide.

1 Select slide 1 in your presentation.

2   Click the New Slide button.

A new slide is added to your project.

3   Drag the new slide to the top of the stack in the slide organizer.

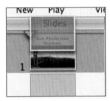

4   Select the text block and press Delete.

5   Select Movies from the Media Browser pop-up menu. If the Media Browser isn't already open, then select the Media Browser and choose Movies.

6 Drag the **SF Tourism.mov** file onto the canvas of slide 1.

7 Select the movie in your canvas and then select the Metrics Inspector.

8 Enter a size of 1024 × 768.

The movie scales to the size of the canvas.

TIP The H.264 compressed movie scales very cleanly. This format requires QuickTime 7 or newer, but works very well. It nicely balances file size and image quality for optimal playback. The file will look good for playback, but will not require a lot of disk space.

9 Enter a position of 0 px for both the X and Y coordinates in the Position fields of the Metrics Inspector.

These coordinates place the upper-left corner of the movie at the upper-left corner of the slide. Because this slide and movie are exactly the same size, the movie completely fills the slide.

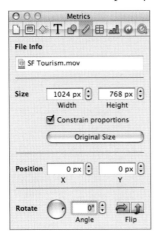

10   Click the Play button to test your presentation's movie introduction and soundtrack.

11   When the movie finishes, press the Esc key to exit your presentation.

Duplicating a Slide

It is a good idea to end your presentation with a title slide that may remain on the screen.

1   Select slide 2 in the slide organizer.

2   Hold down the Option key and drag slide 2 to the bottom of the stack.

The title slide is repeated and added to the bottom of your stack.

3 Press Command-S to save your work so far.

You can check your work by examining **02Presentation1_Stage4.key.**

Keeping Media with Your Presentation

You may have noticed that Keynote took a while to save your presentation file after you added the movie file. This is because Keynote (by default) copies all of the media used in your presentation into the Keynote file. This is a good idea because it simplifies the process of transporting your presentation to another Mac. It means that when you take your Keynote presentation on the road, you have to take only one file with you. Let's check that all of the elements made it into your presentation file for backup.

> **NOTE ▶** Fonts used in a presentation must also be installed on the presentation machine. If you use fonts that are not installed with iWork '06 or that are not OS X system fonts, be sure to install the needed fonts on the new system. Fonts, however, are not saved in the Keynote package. Any fonts used in a Keynote project on one machine need to be installed on any new system where the project will also be used.

1 In Keynote, choose Keynote > Preferences.

2   Click the General button and make sure that all three check boxes in the Saving area are selected.

Checking these options ensures that a backup file is created each time you save. The backup is stored in the same folder as the original. This is a good idea in the rare case that your project file becomes corrupted.

Similarly, it's a good idea to copy both audio and movie files as well as theme images into the document. This is a good idea for both backup purposes and portability of your project file.

3   Close the Preferences window.

> **TIP** If you ever need to access an element from a presentation and don't have access to the original files, you can borrow it from Keynote. Control-click (or right-click if you have a multi-button mouse) the Keynote document and choose Show Package Contents. The folder contains all of the elements of your presentation. You can Option-drag any of the elements to a new folder to copy them.

Lesson Review

1.   What engine drives media playback in Keynote?

2.   Which window allows you easy access to movies, audio files, and photos?

3.   Which iPhoto command allows you to fix common image problems in one click.

4.   Which iLife application allows you to convert an audio file to a Keynote-friendly version?

5.   What inspector can you use if you need to size and position video to fill the screen?

Answers

1. QuickTime allows you to play back a wide variety of image types.

2. The Media Browser window gives you quick access to the iLife applications and the content you create using them.

3. The Enhance button will automatically fix brightness and contrast issues on most images.

4. You can use iTunes to convert audio content into MP3 or AAC files for smooth playback within a presentation.

5. The Metrics Inspector allows specific sizing and positioning of a selected element.

3

Lesson Files   Lessons > Lesson 03 > 03Presentation1_Stage1.key

Time   This lesson takes approximately 1 hour to complete.

Goals   Create builds to reveal text animation on a slide

Create builds to reveal objects on a slide

Create interleaved builds to reveal slide elements concurrently

Create transitions between slides

Add Spotlight comments and keywords for indexing

Configure preferences for smooth playback of a presentation

Run a presentation

Animating and Viewing Your Presentation

Adding animation to your slides is an important step in finalizing a presentation. You can create several types of animation in Keynote. Two of the most common are builds and transitions.

In Keynote, a build allows you to animate the appearance of text or slide elements. You can create dynamic builds that control the order in which information is revealed on a slide. This ordering of information can help your audience, as it directs them where to focus their attention. Keynote harnesses the power of your computer's graphics card to create television-quality animations.

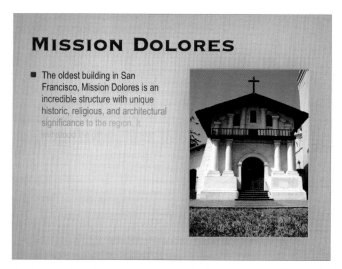

The text on this slide is being animated with a Character Dissolve build. We'll use this animation later in the lesson.

Transitions between slides can also aid your audience. Transitions are meant to signify a change in topic for your audience. Keynote offers several options to choose from, but it is considered good design to limit yourself to just a few in a presentation. Learning how (and when) to add transitions can really enliven your presentation.

Creating Builds to Reveal Text

You can set up your Keynote presentation so that lines of text are revealed to the audience when you click. When revealing text in Keynote, you have several options. There are effects that animate the entire text block as well as those that break up the text by word or character before animating. All text animation is controlled from within the Inspector.

1   Continue with your project from the last lesson or open the file **03Presentation1_Stage1.key** from the DVD-ROM.

2   Click slide 3 in the slide organizer to select it.

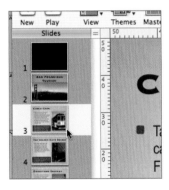

3   In the Inspector, click the Build Inspector button.

4   Click the slide's title "Cable Cars."

5   In the Build Inspector, click Build In. Then choose the following options:

▶   Effect: 2D Effects > Move In

▶   Direction: Right to Left

▶   Duration: 1.50 s

▶   Order is automatically set to 1.

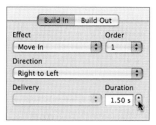

As you change each option, you'll see the thumbnail animation in the inspector update to reflect the new animation.

6   Click the block of bulleted text to select it.

7   In the Build Inspector, click Build In. Then choose the following options:

▶ Effect: Word Effects > Dissolve

▶ Direction: Forward

▶ Delivery: All at Once

▶ Duration: 2.00 s

Note that the order now changes to 2.

As you change each option, the thumbnail animation in the inspector updates again.

8   Select the red text block at the bottom of the page by clicking it.

9   In the Build Inspector, click Build In. Then choose the following options:

▶ Effect: 3D Effects > Flip

▶ Direction: Top to Bottom

▶ Delivery: All at Once

▶ Duration: 1.00 s

10 Apply the same settings to slides 4, 5, 6, and 7. Alternately, you can skip ahead and open the file **03Presentation1_Stage2.key** from the DVD-ROM.

11 Press Command-S to save your work.

You have now animated the text on the majority of your slides. This will help control the flow of information (by preventing the audience from reading ahead). It also adds visual "pop" to reinforce your points.

Creating a Sequence Build to Reveal a Table

Keynote also offers flexible build options for other elements in your presentation. For example, using transitions on table cells can help enliven calculations.

By revealing the information in stages, you can guide the viewer through the data.

1   Click slide 8 in the slide organizer to select it. This slide should contain a table.

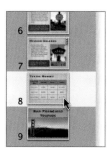

2   Click the slide's title "Travel Budget."

3   In the Build Inspector, click Build In. Then choose the following options:

▶   Effect: 2D Effects > Move In

▶   Direction: Right to Left

▶   Duration: 1.50 s

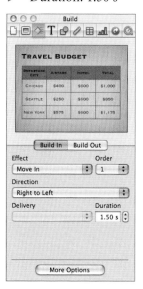

4   Select the table on the slide canvas.

5   In the Build Inspector, click Build In. Then choose the following options:

▶   Effect: 2D Effects > Scale

▶   Direction: Down

▶   Delivery: By Row (This option reveals information one row at a time.)

▶   Duration: 1.00 s

TIP ▶ To animate objects entering the screen, use Build In. To animate objects leaving the screen, use Build Out.

6   Save your work.

Creating Interleaved Builds

So far, you have created builds that progress linearly from one to another when you click. Keynote also offers the ability to interleave elements, so the animations happen concurrently. For instance, you might have a line of text and an image that you want to reveal at the same time. Let's examine a basic application of this technique.

1   Select slide 2 in the slide organizer.

2   Click the slide's title "San Francisco Tourism" so you can add a text animation.

3 In the Build Inspector, click Build In. Then choose the following options:

▶ Effect: Character Effects > Scale Big

▶ Direction: From Edges

▶ Delivery: All at Once

▶ Duration: 2.50 s

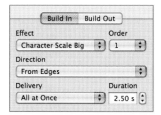

4 Select the photo on the slide. You are going to animate the photo scaling so it appears dramatically on the slide.

5 In the Build Inspector, click Build In. Then choose the following options:

▶ Effect: 2D Effects > Scale

▶ Direction: Down

▶ Duration: 2.50 s

In the animation thumbnail, you'll see that the photo is added *after* the text. You are going to change that.

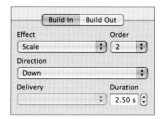

6 Click the More Options button at the bottom of the Build Inspector.

The Build Order drawer opens and allows you to specify the order of the builds on your slide.

TIP▶ You can drag items to change their order.

7 In the Build Order drawer, click item 2 so it is highlighted.

8 In the pop-up menu under Start Build, choose Automatically with build 1.

This option makes two objects appear at the same time. You can also specify the amount of time specified in the Delay field. The two builds must occur consecutively in the Build Order list.

The On Click option in this menu initiates the build when you click any key or the mouse button. The Automatically after build [#] option initiates the build after the build number indicated (which is always the previous build). You can also specify the amount of delay between the two builds.

9 Select slide 2 in the slide organizer and choose Edit > Copy, or press Command-C.

The animated title slide is now copied to your clipboard.

10 Select slide 8 in the slide organizer and choose Edit > Paste, or press Command-V.

The animated title slide is now pasted into your presentation for a second instance. There are two copies of the title slide at the end—one with animation and one without.

Look closely in the upper-right corner of the slide's thumbnail in the Navigator. The three dots indicate animation.

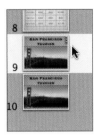

11 Select slide 10 in the Navigator and press Delete to remove the static slide from your presentation.

You now have animated title slides at the start and end of your presentation.

12 Save your work.

You can compare your presentation to the file **03Presentation1_Stage3.key** from the DVD-ROM.

Watching the Presentation So Far

We're not done, but we've accomplished quite a bit. Let's check our progress so far and see how the slides animate. You'll still need to add transitions between slides, but all things in time.

1 Select slide 1 in the slide organizer.

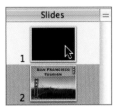

2 Click Play in the toolbar (or choose View > Play Slideshow).

NOTE ▶ Clicking Play will run the slideshow starting with the currently selected slide. To start the slideshow from the beginning (if the first slide is not selected), hold down the Option key while clicking Play.

3 Click the mouse button or spacebar advance to the next slide.

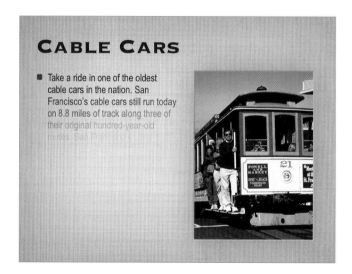

NOTE ▶ You can control the playback of the movie on the first slide from the keyboard. Press K to stop playback. Press K again to resume playback. Hold J to rewind the movie. Hold L to fast-forward the movie.

4 Click through the entire movie slideshow.

5 To exit the slideshow, press Q or the Esc key.

Creating Transitions Between Slides

After watching your presentation, you should be pleased with your efforts so far. However, your show probably felt a bit jarring as it went from slide to slide. Adding transitions can help polish a show and add visual interest for your audience.

When you select a slide, you can choose a transition for exiting that slide. Keynote offers several 2D and 3D effects, many of which are not available in competing programs. In fact, the proper use of transitions can help set your presentation apart from the competition (visually at least).

1   Select slide 1 in the slide organizer.

2   Select the Slide Inspector and click Transition. Then choose the following options:

▶   Effect: 2D Effects > Fade Through Color (By default it is set to black, which is fine for this transition.)

▶   Duration: 2.00 s

▶   Start Transition: On Click

3 Select slide 2 in the slide organizer.

4 In the Slide Inspector, choose the following options:

▶ Effect: 3D Effects > Flip

▶ Duration: 1.50 s

▶ Direction: Top to Bottom

▶ Start Transition: On Click

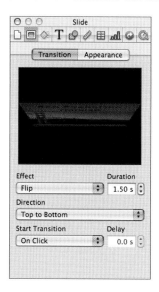

You can add transitions to multiple slides simultaneously to speed up the process.

5 Select slide 3 in the Navigator. Hold down the Shift key and click slide 7.

Slides 3 to 7 should now be highlighted in yellow to show that they are selected.

6   In the Slide Inspector, choose the following options:

▶   Effect: 3D Effects > Revolving Door

▶   Duration: 1.50 s

▶   Direction: Right

▶   Start Transition: On Click

NOTE ▶ The triangle in the corner of a slide's thumbnail in the slide organizer indicates that you have added a transition to that slide.

7   Select slide 8 in the slide organizer.

8   In the Slide Inspector, choose the following options:

▶   Effect: 3D Effects > Fall

▶   Duration: 1.50 s

▶   Start Transition: On Click

9   Save your work.

Indexing Your Presentation with Spotlight

Starting with OS X Tiger, Apple has improved the ability to search the contents of your hard drive. By using Spotlight, you can enter keywords to refine a search. This process can be very fast as Spotlight can index your system. The more information you give it, the more accurately your files can be indexed.

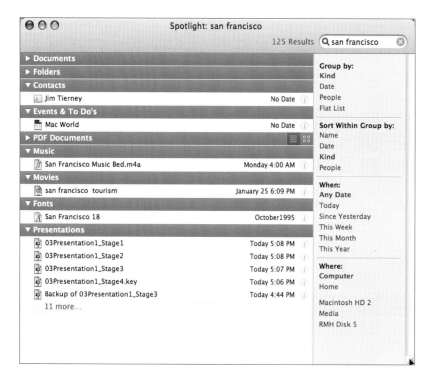

Keynote 3 allows you to accurately index your presentation files for easy searching later. You can add your name, the title of your presentation, keywords, and comments to a Keynote presentation. Then you can use Spotlight to search for presentations containing that information.

1   Open the Document Inspector.

2   Click the Spotlight button.

3   Enter the information you want to use for searches:

▶   Author: Type your name.

▶   Title: San Francisco Tourism.

▶   Keywords: Enter titles of slides or major topics.

▶   Comments: Describe what the presentation was created for.

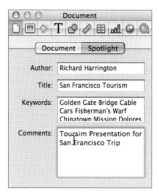

4   Save your work.

The next time you search with Spotlight, your presentation will be easier to find.

Configuring Preferences for Smooth Playback

Factors such as the quality of your graphics card and monitor (or projector) resolution can greatly affect the appearance of your presentation upon playback. Before running your presentation, you may need to tweak a few options to enhance the playback quality of your presentation.

Freeing Up RAM

When giving a presentation, it is a good idea to close any applications that are open, but not needed. This will make the most of your computer's RAM and reduce playback errors.

TIP A quick way to cycle among open applications is to press Command-Tab. A panel appears on your screen bearing icons of all the open applications on your system. While you continue to press the Command key, each time you press Tab, a new open application is highlighted. While still holding down the Command key, you can press Q to quit an open application that does not have unsaved documents open. If a document does have open documents that need to be saved, switch to that application and manually close and save your documents.

Scaling Slides Up

Oftentimes the resolution of your slideshow will not match that of your playback device, resulting in a black border around the outside of your presentation because there is not enough slide information to fill the screen. There are two methods for solving this problem: You can fit the presentation to the display only during playback, or you can change the monitor resolution.

To fit the presentation to the display only during playback, follow these steps:

1 Choose Keynote > Preferences.

2 Click the Slideshow button.

3 Select the "Scale slides up to fit display" check box.

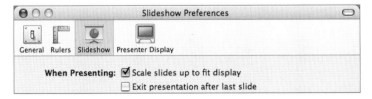

This option does not change the slide size of your Keynote document. It simply scales the slides up during playback to fit the display. This can result in some loss of image quality due to resampling.

4   Close the Slideshow Preferences window to apply the change.

   NOTE ▶ If your presentation is larger than the playback screen, Keynote automatically scales your presentation down regardless of the state of the Scale slides check box.

Scaling Slides Up: Another Approach

Slides may play back slowly if you turn on the "Scale slides up to fit display" option. An alternative is to change the display resolution.

1   Choose Keynote > Preferences.

2   Deselect the "Scale slides up to fit display" check box.

3   Click the Open Display Preferences button.

4   Choose a smaller screen resolution, ideally one that matches the resolution of your Keynote document.

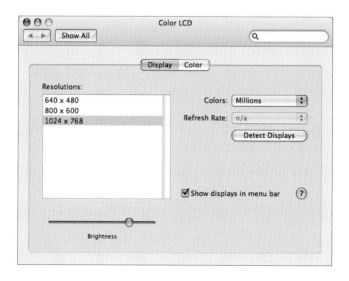

5   Close the System Preferences window and return to Keynote.

6   Close the Slideshow Preferences window.

Preventing Transitions from Being Clipped

If your playback display is smaller than a slide, part of the slide may be clipped during transitions. This happens for both the Cube and Flip transitions. This also happens if you select the "Scale slides up to fit display" check box.

1   Choose Keynote > Preferences.

2   Click the Slideshow button.

3   Select the "Reduce Cube transitions to avoid clipping" check box.

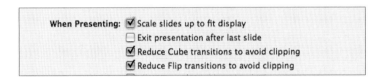

4   Select the "Reduce Flip transitions to avoid clipping" check box.

5   Close the Slideshow Preferences window to apply the change.

Changing the Mouse Pointer Behavior

Generally, your mouse pointer shouldn't appear onscreen during a presentation, except when you're clicking a hyperlink or controlling a movie. In Keynote 3, you can set preferences so that the pointer appears only on slides that contain hyperlinks or only when the mouse is moved.

1   Choose Keynote > Preferences.

2   Click the Slideshow button.

3   Choose one of the Show pointer options.

▶   Show pointer only on slides with hyperlinks or movies: This is a good option if you are using a mouse to advance your slides and you don't want to accidentally activate the cursor.

▶   Show pointer when the mouse moves: This option give you maximum control and keeps the mouse cursor visible.

> ⦿ Show pointer only on slides with hyperlinks or movies
> ◯ Show pointer when the mouse moves

4   Close the Slideshow Preferences window to apply the change.

> **TIP** ▶ While presenting a slideshow, you can show or hide the pointer by pressing the C key.

Using Exposé and Dashboard During a Presentation

Mac OS X offers Exposé, which you can use to quickly view all open windows, and Dashboard, which provides widgets that you can customize for specialty tasks and desktop activities. While both are very useful, they can have a negative impact on the playback quality of your presentation, so for best results, you'll want them turned off.

1   Choose Keynote > Preferences.

2   Click the Slideshow button.

3   Make sure that the "Allow Exposé, Dashboard and others to use screen" check box is not selected.

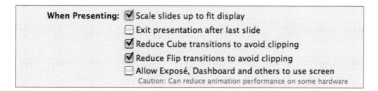

4   Close the Slideshow Preferences window to apply the change.

Running Your Presentation

Now that your system is configured, it's time to run your presentation. This will give you a chance to see all of your work in action. If you have been following along for the past three lessons, your presentation should be ready to go. If you've skipped some steps, then open the file **03Presentation1_Stage4.key** from the DVD-ROM.

We'll explore using a second display or a projector in the next lesson. For now, we'll focus on playback commands that work regardless of display setup.

1 Hold down the Option key and click the Play button in the toolbar.

   This starts the presentation from the first slide.

2 When the movie finishes, press the spacebar to advance to the next build. In this case, it will be a transition to the next slide.

There are several other ways to advance from build to build (these short-cuts match other presentation software packages). You can click the mouse button (left button on a Mighty Mouse) or press the Return, N, Down Arrow, Page Down, or Right Arrow key.

NOTE ▸ To advance to the next slide (regardless of whether there are still stages left in the build), press right bracket (]), Shift–Page Down, or Shift–Down Arrow.

3   Continue to click through your presentation until you are on the Chinatown District slide.

4   Click three times to bring up the title, bullet, and tip elements. Do not advance to the next slide. You are now on slide 5, but are going to skip a slide in the presentation.

   TIP ▸ If you need to go back to the previous slide, press P, Left Arrow, Up Arrow, Shift–Up Arrow, Page Up, or the Delete key.

5   Press the number 7 on your keyboard; this calls up the slide switcher.

   The slide switcher is active at the bottom of the screen.

   TIP ▸ It is a good idea to keep a printout of your slide outline (with slide numbers) with you while presenting. You may need to jump around during a presentation, especially if your allotted time for the presentation changes.

6   Press Enter to switch to the selected slide.

   You can change which slide is selected in the slide switcher by using the keyboard. Use the following shortcuts to navigate the slide switcher:

   ▸   Go to the next slide in the slide switcher by pressing the plus sign (+) or equal sign (=).

▶   Go to the previous slide in the slide switcher by pressing the minus sign (–).

▶   Go to the selected slide and close the slide switcher by pressing the Return or Enter key.

▶   Close the slide switcher (without changing slides) by pressing the Esc key.

7   Continue advancing through your remaining slides and builds until you reach the end of your presentation.

8   To exit the slideshow, press the Esc key.

You also can exit a slideshow by pressing the Q, period, or Command-period keys.

Congratulations! You've successfully created and viewed an elaborate presentation that harnessed audio and video. You also created builds and transitions to help control the flow of information.

TIP ▶ To see a list of keyboard shortcuts you can use while you're giving a presentation, press the Help, question mark (?), or forward slash (/) key during the presentation.

Pausing and Resuming a Slideshow

It is very common to need to switch gears during a presentation. For instance, you may want to switch to another application to show off a document or to access a file at the Finder level. Keynote offers several ways to pause a presentation:

▶   To pause a presentation and display the current slide, press the F key (as in freeze). To resume the presentation, press the F key or spacebar.

▶   To pause the presentation and display a black screen, press the B key. To resume the presentation, press the B key or spacebar.

▶ To pause the presentation and display a white screen, press the W key. To resume the presentation, press the W key or spacebar.

▶ To pause the presentation and hide Keynote, press the H key. To resume the presentation, click the Keynote icon in the Dock.

Troubleshooting Your Presentation

Most likely, the presentation ran perfectly on your computer—the video played back smoothly, and all builds worked properly. The following information is offered in case you hit a snag or if you are presenting on a different machine than you built the presentation on. Hopefully you won't need this information, but it's still good to have it.

If Transition or Build Effects Don't Work

Certain effects like Dissolve, Scale, and Swoosh require an advanced graphics card. These effects rely on Core Image technology (another component of Mac OS X), which ties to your graphics card. If certain effects don't play back smoothly, be sure to check the Slide and Build Inspectors. Unsupported effects will be listed below "Effects that can't play on this computer" in the Effects pop-up menu.

If Slides Play Poorly

If your slideshow stutters or if artifacts appear, first be sure that all media is running on a hard disk drive and not on removable media like a DVD or USB thumb drive. If media speed is not the issue, then the problem could be insufficient VRAM, projector setup issues, or improper screen refresh rate.

Keynote requires a minimum of 8 MB of VRAM (video random access memory) to play transition animations. More complex animations (such as some object builds) can need at least 32 MB of VRAM. The amount of VRAM available is a feature of your graphics card. If you think you are having memory issues, check out how much VRAM you have.

1   In the Finder, from the Apple menu, choose About This Mac.

2   Click the More Info button to launch the System Profiler application.

3   In the System Profiler window, in the Hardware category, click Graphics/Displays.

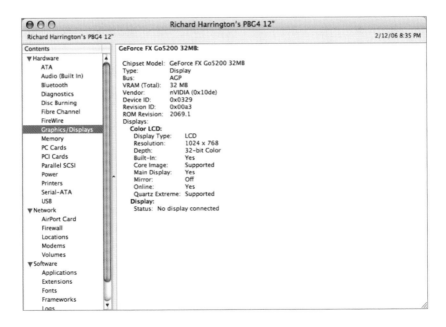

4   If your computer has less than 32 MB of VRAM and your slideshow has a playback issue, open the Displays pane of System Preferences and try the following:

▶   Turn on video mirroring.

▶   Set your displays to a lower resolution. Lower screen resolutions use less VRAM.

▶   Set your displays to use fewer colors. You can use Thousands instead of Millions as a last effort solution.

NOTE ▶ Even if you have 32 MB of VRAM (or more), you may still see occasional choppiness at very-high screen resolutions. The good news is that most Macs ship with more powerful graphics cards.

Lesson Review

1.   Where do you control builds?

2.   To combine two builds into a single action, what button do you click?

3.   True or false: Keynote offers both 2D and 3D slide transitions.

4.   How can you index your presentation for easier searches using Spotlight?

5.   What keys do you press to pause a presentation and hide Keynote?

Answers

1.   The Build Inspector offers complete control over build options.

2.   Click the More Options button to access timing controls.

3.   True. Keynote offers more than 20 advanced slide transitions. You must however have enough VRAM to access all of them.

4.   In the Documents Inspector, click the Spotlight button. You can then add keywords and other information for the document.

5.   Pressing the H key will hide the presentation and exit you to the Finder. Clicking the Keynote icon in the Dock will resume the presentation.

4

Lesson Files	Lessons > Lesson 04 > 04Table.doc
	Lessons > Lesson 04 > 04Almonic Senior Investments PPT Slides.pdf
	Lessons > Lesson 04 > 04Almonic Senior Investments.ppt
	Lessons > Lesson 04 > 04Presentation Complete.key
Time	This lesson takes approximately 90 minutes to complete.
Goals	Import a PowerPoint presentation into Keynote
	Use Pages to convert a Word document into an iWork-compatible format and add it to a Keynote presentation
	Modify and enhance imported content
	Use timings and automatic builds
	Add comments
	Customize Presenter mode
	Rehearse the presentation

Lesson 4

Converting a PowerPoint Presentation

Keynote has been built from the ground up to take advantage of the many powerful graphics features in OS X. Many professional presenters have switched to Keynote for its rich media playback abilities and expert handling of text and bullet animation. Despite all of these benefits, not everyone uses Keynote. It's thus important that Keynote be compatible with other presentation methods.

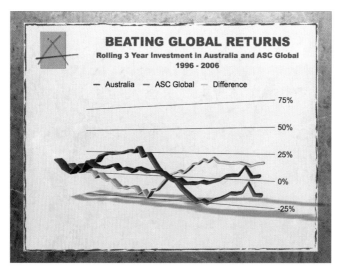

Keynote allows you to enhance charts and use 3D space to improve their look.

Keynote can export both PDF and PowerPoint files, so you can easily share your Keynote presentations with people using these other applications. Even more important, you can open an existing PowerPoint document and enhance it with the many features of Keynote. This allows you to take an existing presentation and modify it further or work with a template. The conversion process is relatively easy, and the vast majority of features import. Most important, the data and text are editable so you can continue to modify your presentation. In this lesson, you will modify an existing PowerPoint presentation. You'll modify slides and content to improve the overall appearance of the presentation.

Importing a PowerPoint Presentation

Bringing a PowerPoint presentation into Keynote allows you to modify and edit the content. The conversion process is as easy as opening a file.

1   If Keynote is not already running, launch it.

2   Choose File > Open.

3   Navigate to the file **04Almonic Senior Investments.ppt**.

4   Click Open.

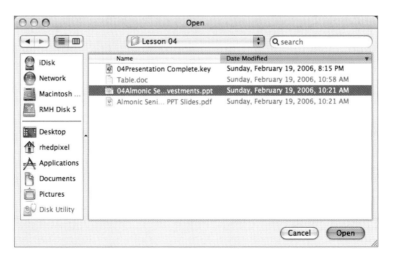

Keynote converts the file and names it "Untitled." The original PowerPoint document remains unmodified on your hard drive.

5   Choose File> Save As and name the file **04Presentation Stage 01.key** and save it to your hard drive.

You need to resize the new document to optimize it for the screen. The converted PowerPoint file imported into Keynote at 720 × 540 pixels. This is an uncommon size, and it is better to choose a more standard resolution to match a projector.

6   Select the Document Inspector.

7   Click the Slide Size menu and choose 1024 × 768.

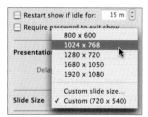

Your slides scale up to match the new size.

8   Press Command-S to save your document.

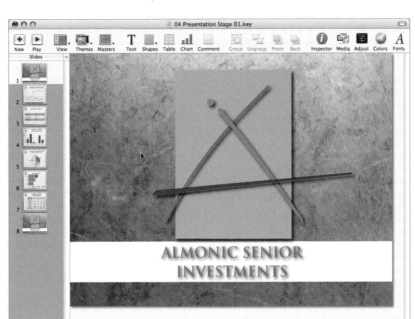

NOTE ▶ On the DVD, you'll find a PDF file called **04Almonic Senior Investments PPT Slides.pdf** that you can open for reference. This document shows you how the slides looked when originally created in PowerPoint. Additionally, your Mac may have shipped with a trial version of Microsoft office. You can open the original document on the DVD (**04Almonic Senior Investments.ppt**) using Microsoft PowerPoint as well.

Animating the Title Slide

The first slide in our presentation could benefit from some animation. This will help capture your audience's attention at the start of your presentation. Keynote offers several build animations that can be used to enhance the slide.

1   Select slide 1 in the slide organizer.

2   Select the Build Inspector.

3   Select the logo in the canvas.

4   From the Effect pop-up menu, choose Scale, and from the Direction pop-up menu, choose Down.

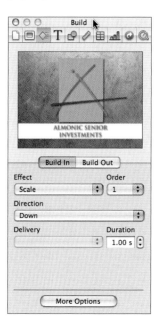

5   Select the white bar in the canvas.

6 From the Effect menu, choose Dissolve.

Currently the two animations happen sequentially. You can set the animations to occur simultaneously.

7 Click the More Options button at the bottom of the inspector.

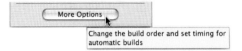

This panel allows you to adjust the timing of build animations.

8 From the Build Order list, select Item #1.

9 From the Start Build menu, select Automatically after transition.

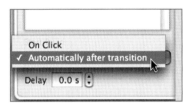

10 From the Build Order list, select Item #2.

11 From the Start Build menu, select Automatically with build 1.

12 Click the slide thumbnail in the inspector to see a preview of the animation.

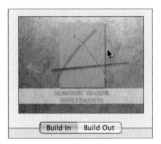

13 Click the Slide Inspector button and then click Transition.

14 From the Effect pop-up menu, choose 3D Effects: Doorway and set the duration to 1.50 s.

15 Click the slide thumbnail in the inspector to see a preview of the animation.

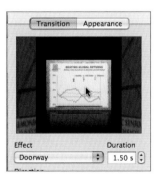

16 Press Command-S to save your document.

Cleaning Up a Chart

Imported charts may need a little cleanup. The process is simple.

1 Select slide 2 in the slide organizer.

Some extraneous information was imported with the slide—notice the several overlapping lines at 0%. Also notice the illegible legend at the bottom of the chart. Problems like these are easy to fix.

2 Select the chart in the canvas.

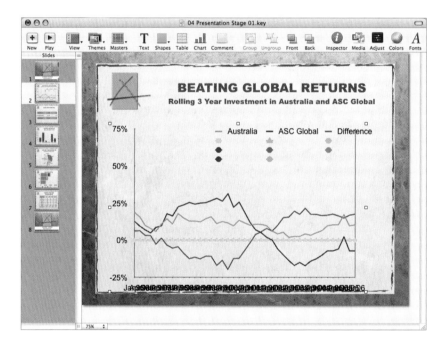

3 Select the Chart Inspector and click the Edit Data button.

We need to edit the chart data to see why all of the zeros appear in the chart.

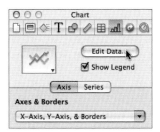

The Chart Data Editor opens, but information is partially cut off and you need to expand the window to see it.

4 Grab the corner of the Chart Data Editor and drag down and to the right to enlarge it.

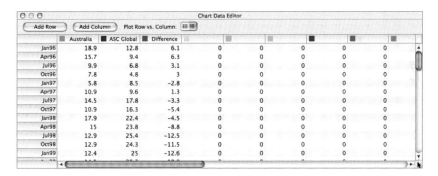

	Australia	ASC Global	Difference					
Jan96	18.9	12.8	6.1	0	0	0	0	0
Apr96	15.7	9.4	6.3	0	0	0	0	0
Jul96	9.9	6.8	3.1	0	0	0	0	0
Oct96	7.8	4.8	3	0	0	0	0	0
Jan97	5.8	8.5	-2.8	0	0	0	0	0
Apr97	10.9	9.6	1.3	0	0	0	0	0
Jul97	14.5	17.8	-3.3	0	0	0	0	0
Oct97	10.9	16.3	-5.4	0	0	0	0	0
Jan98	17.9	22.4	-4.5	0	0	0	0	0
Apr98	15	23.8	-8.8	0	0	0	0	0
Jul98	12.9	25.4	-12.5	0	0	0	0	0
Oct98	12.9	24.3	-11.5	0	0	0	0	0
Jan99	12.4	25	-12.6	0	0	0	0	0

There are several empty columns that contain only zeros. These need to be deleted.

5   Click the header of the yellow column to select it.

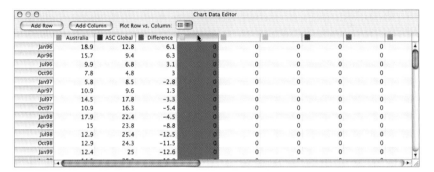

6   Drag the scroll bar at the bottom of the Chart Data Editor window so you see the last column of zeros.

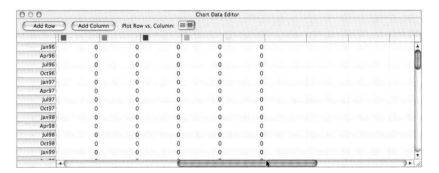

7   Hold down the Shift key and click the header of the last column filled with zeros.

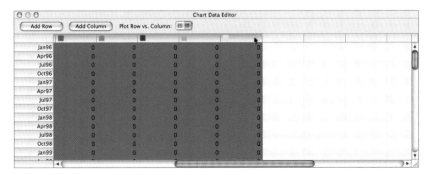

8   Choose Edit > Delete to remove the extra columns of information.

The other conversion issue we need to address is the illegible legend beneath the x-axis.

9   Close the Chart Data Editor.

10   Click the dense text area at the bottom of slide 2.

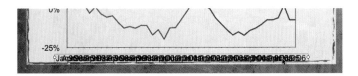

11   Working in the Labels, Ticks, & Grids area of the Chart Inspector, from the X-Axis menu choose Diagonal Labels.

This will reorient the labels and make them easier to read in a small space.

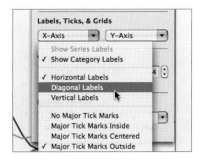

The text in the legend is still too large and overlaps itself.

12   Click the Fonts button in the document toolbar to open the Font panel.

13   Change the font size to 12 points; then close the Font panel.

14 Click the legend near the top on the slide and drag it so it is centered on the slide canvas.

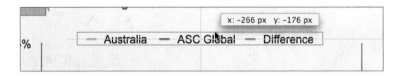

Yellow alignment guides will pop up when the text is centered.

Enhancing a Chart

Now that the slide is cleaned up, you can enhance it. Keynote offers several 3D options as well as graphic choices that can improve a chart. To help the viewer better understand the data, you will convert the chart to 3D. You will also enhance its appearance to better match your slides.

1 Click the chart in the canvas to select it.

2 Select the Chart Inspector. Then click the Chart Type thumbnail to open a pop-up menu.

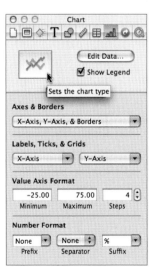

3 Select the fifth icon in the second column to create a 3D line chart.

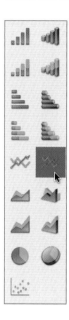

The conversion may take a few seconds. When finished, the chart will need a little enhancement to make it more readable and better match your other slides.

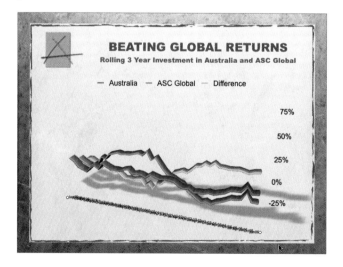

4 In the Chart Inspector, click 3D Scene.

The 3D Scene pane of the Chart Inspector lets you adjust the graphical 3D properties of the chart such as the depth, angle, and shadows.

5 Modify the lighting style, chart depth, and viewing angle of the chart by using the sliders and directional wheel. Adjust to taste.

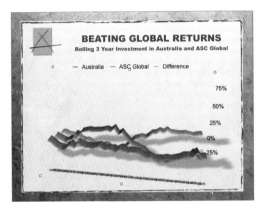

6 Click the Axis button in the Chart Inspector.

The x-axis label is difficult to read, so we will remove it.

7 From the X-Axis menu under Labels, Ticks, and Grids, choose Show Category Labels to turn off the option.

Instead of listing the year information in the x-axis label, we're going to add the information at the top of the slide.

8 Double-click the slide title and place the insertion point at the end of the second line. Press Return to add a third line of text. Type *1996–2006*.

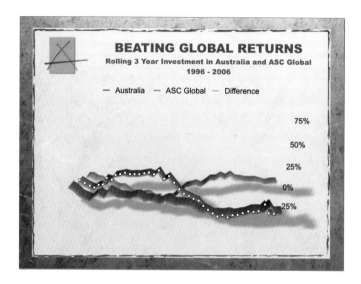

We can now color the chart to match our logo.

9   Double-click the blue line in the chart.

10 Select the Graphic Inspector.

You'll see that the Fill color well matches the blue in the chart.

11 Click the color well to open the Colors window.

12 Click the magnifying glass icon to activate the color sampler. Click a blue area in the logo to match the blue.

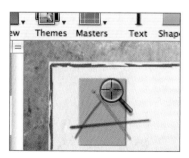

13 Change the other two lines of the chart to match the red and gold in the logo.

14 Ensure that the chart is clear and easy to read.

Examine the viewing angle as well as depth and shadow settings. Be sure you haven't accidentally changed the meaning of the chart with a perspective error. Notice how the two figures here present the same information in very different lights. The one on the right is more truthful.

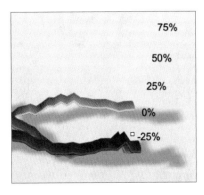 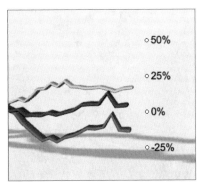

15 To further improve readability, turn on the gridlines for the y-axis. Select the Chart Inspector and click the Axis button.

16 From the Y-Axis menu under Labels, Ticks, and Grids, choose Show Gridlines.

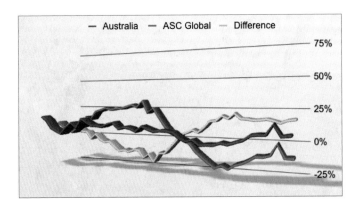

Animating a Chart

Now that the chart is built, we can animate it. This will allow you to reveal the slide data one series at a time. This can be useful to keep your audience's attention as well as to control the flow of information.

1   Select the chart on slide 2. Then select the Build Inspector.

2   From the Effect menu, choose Wipe.

3   From the Direction menu, choose Left to Right.

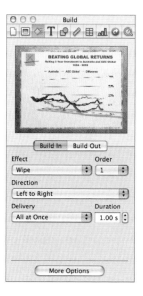

4   From the Delivery pop-up menu, choose By Series.

This option will animate each element in the chart, first the gridlines and then each data series.

5   Set the duration to 2.00 seconds.

Watch the animation preview in the inspector. Notice how the background and grid wipes onto the screen first. Generally, you'll want this part of the chart already on the page so you'll remove it from the animation.

6   Choose 2 from the Build from menu; leave the Build to menu set to Last.

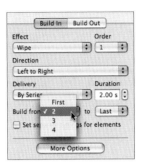

Now that the chart is animated, you can choose a transition to move from this page in the presentation to the next.

7   Select the Slide Inspector and click Transition. Then choose the following options:

▶   Transition Effect: 3D Effects: Page Flip

▶   Direction: Left

▶   Duration: 2.00 s

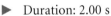

8   Press Command-S to save your document.

Enhancing a Table

A chart is not the only thing that can be animated in Keynote. You can use a build animation to reveal the contents of a table as well.

1 Select slide 3 in the slide organizer.

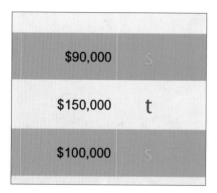

The table imported cleanly except for the up and down triangles. The original table used red and yellow triangles, but these did not convert properly when the file was opened in Keynote. These triangles were originally created using a font. While we could simply select them and change the font, we do have other options.

2 Launch System Preferences by choosing Apple Menu > System Preferences.

3 Click the International icon in the top row.

4 Click Input Menu and select the Character Palette check box.

The Character Palette allows you to visually browse all of the characters of a font. It also allows you quick access to specialty symbols such as arrows, currency symbols, and international characters.

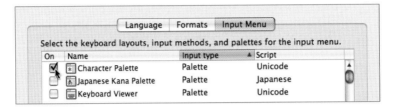

5   Close System Preferences by clicking the red dot in the top-left corner.

6   Click the Input Menu icon (it looks like a flag) in your menu bar and choose Show Character Palette.

    Depending upon the country you are in (and the language you have chosen), the flag will vary.

7   Triple-click the yellow *s* to select it in the top row of the table.

8   Make the Character Palette active by clicking it, and then click the Miscellaneous category.

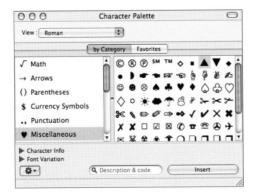

9   Double-click the triangle icon that points up to insert it into the table cell.

10 Select the second yellow *s* and repeat the substitution.

11 Select the red *t* and replace it with the downward pointing triangle.

 The row heights are all different, but this is easy to fix.

12 Select all of the cells in the table by clicking and dragging.

13 Choose the Table Inspector and click Table.

14 Set the row height to 100 px.

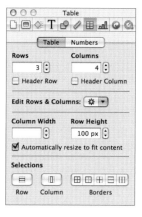
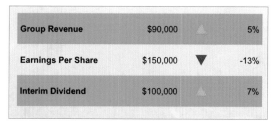

15 Select the Build Inspector and then choose the following options from the Build In area:

> ▶   Effect: Flip

> ▶   Direction: Top to Bottom

> ▶   Delivery: By Row

> ▶   Duration: 1.00 s

 The chart is animated; you will now add a transition to the next slide.

16 Select the Slide Inspector and click Transition. Then choose the following options:

- ▶ Transition Effect: 3D Effects: Page Flip
- ▶ Direction: Down
- ▶ Duration: 2.00 s

17 Save your project.

Animating a Bar Chart

You can set up a bar chart to grow over time. You also can use 3D perspective to improve your chart's readability for the audience.

1 Select slide 4 in the slide organizer.

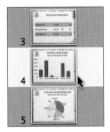

2 Select the chart in the canvas. Then select the Chart Inspector.

3 From the Chart Type menu, choose the first 3D option.

The chart is rendered in 3D, but it is using a flat gray color, which you will change.

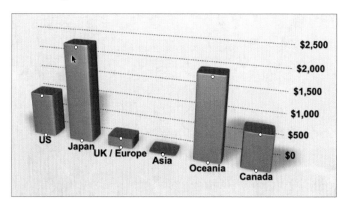

4   Click one of the vertical bars.

All of the bars become selected.

5   Select the Graphic Inspector; then click the Fill color well to open the Colors window.

6   With the magnifying glass, select the red in the logo to color the chart.

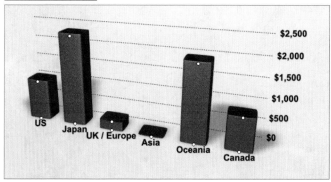

7 Select the Build Inspector and click Build In. Then choose the following options:

▶ Effect: Dissolve

▶ Delivery: By Element in Series

▶ Duration: 1.00 s

▶ Choose 2 from the Build from menu; leave the Build to menu set to Last.

8 Click the More Options button.

9 In the Build Order list, select Series Elements.

10 For Start Build, choose Automatically after prior build; for Delay, choose 1.0 s.

11 Select the Slide Inspector and click Transition. Then choose the following options:

▶ Transition Effect: 3D Effects: Page Flip

▶ Direction: Up

▶ Duration: 2.00 s

12 Press Command-S to save your document.

Animating a Pie Chart

To continue our practice of builds and transitions, let's move to the next slide. Pie charts can also be animated to reveal one slice of the pie at a time.

1 Select slide 5 in the slide organizer.

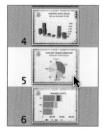

2 Select the chart in the canvas. Then select the Chart Inspector.

3 In the Chart Type menu, choose the 3D pie chart option at the bottom.

The chart is rendered in 3D, but it is small and needs more colors to better show details.

4 While holding down the Shift key, grab the upper-right corner of the pie chart and drag toward the upper-right corner of your screen. Release the mouse button when the pie chart is large enough to fill the empty area at the bottom of the slide.

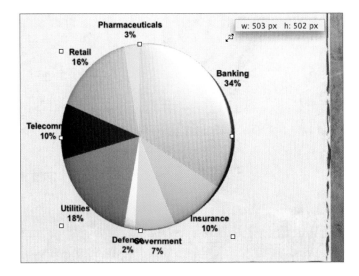

5 In the Chart Inspector, click 3D Scene and drag the 3D Rotation Angle wheel adjust the viewing angle to taste.

6 Increase the depth of the chart by dragging the Chart Depth slider to the right.

7 Click Series in the Chart Inspector.

You now need to add a legend to the chart to help identify the data in the chart.

8 Select the Show Legend check box.

9 Position the legend on the left of the screen.

10 Open the Font panel and change the legend font to Arial Bold to match other slides. Set the point size to 24.

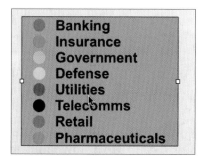

11 Select the chart; then open the Data Point Settings menu in the Data Point Label area and deselect the Show Series Name option.

12 Select the Graphic Inspector.

13 Click the pie wedge next to 16%.

14 Click the Fill color well to open the Colors window.

15 Click the Crayons tab to access preset colors and change the color to Maraschino.

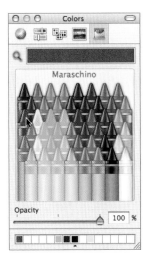

16 Continue changing colors for the other wedges in the pie chart. Close the Colors window when you've changed them all.

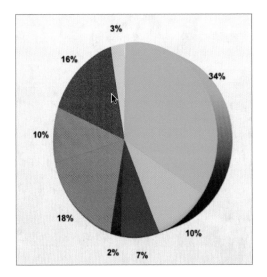

17 In the Build Inspector, click Build In. Then choose the following options to create a build animation for the pie chart:

▶ Effect: Scale

▶ Direction: Up

▶ Delivery: By Wedge

▶ Duration: 1.00 s

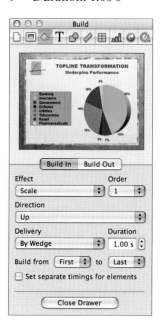

18 Click the More Options button.

19 In the Build Order list, select Other Wedges.

20 From the Start Build menu, choose Automatically after prior build.

21 For Delay, choose 0.5 s.

22 Select the Slide Inspector and click the Transition tab. Then choose the following options:

▶ Effect: 3D Effects: Page Flip

▶ Direction: Right

▶ Duration: 2.00 s

23 Press Command-S to save your document.

Changing the Style of a Chart

Not only can you change the style of a chart to make it appear 3D, but you can change its entire method of charting. By switching the way that the data is presented, you can make the data easier for your audience to understand. Changing the charting method will result in an entirely different look.

1   Select Slide 6 in the slide organizer.

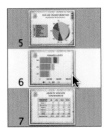

2   Select the chart in the canvas. Then select the Chart Inspector.

3   For Value Access Format, change the maximum from 600000.00 to
     450000.00.

     This setting reduces the empty area on the chart by decreasing the range
     of charted information.

4   Set the chart type to the 3D area chart option. It's the seventh one in the
     second column.

5   Increase the depth of the chart by dragging the Chart Depth slider to
     the right.

6 In the 3D Scene pane of the Chart Inspector, adjust the viewing angle of the pie chart to taste.

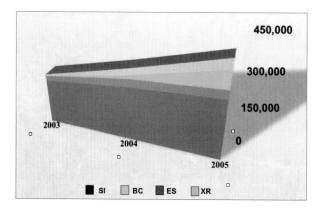

7 Double-click one of the years on the x-axis so you can change the font used for the axis labels.

8 Open the Font panel and change the x-axis label font to Arial Bold to match the other slides. Set the point size to 24.

9 Click Series in the Chart Inspector.

You need to add information to the slide so the data is clearer to the audience.

10 Select the Show Legend check box.

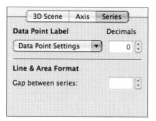

A second legend appears on the slide. This legend is tied to the chart (so changes in the chart will affect it). The other one, currently at the bottom of the slide, was added as part of the importing process. You want only the legend you created in Keynote.

11 Shift-click to select the multiple elements of the original legend.

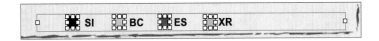

Then press Delete to delete this legend.

12 Drag the Keynote-created legend to the bottom of the slide.

13 Change the font in the legend to Arial bold.

14 Drag the legend to center it on the page using Smart Guides.

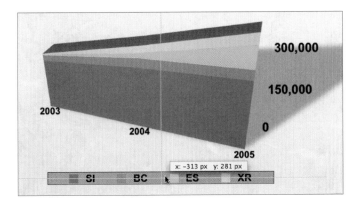

15 Change the colors in the Area Chart using the Graphics Inspector.

Use the same techniques as earlier in the lesson and match colors to the logo.

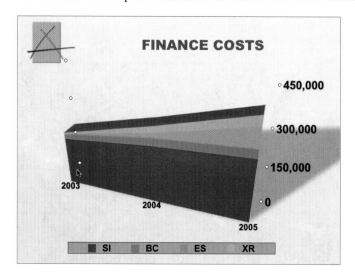

16 In the Build Inspector, click Build In. Then choose the following options:

▶ Effect: Wipe

▶ Direction: Left to Right

▶ Delivery: By Series

▶ Duration: 2.00 s

▶ Choose 2 from the Build from menu; leave the Build to menu set to Last.

17 Click the More Options button.

18 In the Build Order list, select Chart Series.

19 For Start Build, choose Automatically after prior build.

20 For Delay, choose 1.5 s.

21 Select the Slide Inspector and click Transition. Then choose the following options:

▶ Effect: 3D Effects: Page Flip

▶ Direction: Down

▶ Duration: 2.00 s

22 Press Command-S to save your document.

Replacing the Content of a Slide

While building a presentation, you may need to replace the content of a slide with new information. This is especially common when working on a group presentation. New slide content may be provided in several forms. One common form is as a Microsoft Word file. Although Keynote cannot open a Word document, you can open it using Pages.

Pages is included with the iWork suite, and it is designed for word processing and page layout tasks. We will explore Pages in great depth later in this book. For now, we'll use it just to convert a table contained in a Word document into a format we can use.

1 Launch the Pages application (you can do this by clicking its icon in the Dock or launching it from your Application folder). The Template Chooser appears with a list of available Pages templates.

2   Click the Open an Existing File button.

3   Navigate to the project folder for the lesson and open the file **04Table.doc**.

The file opens in Pages as an untitled document. The original Word document is untouched on your hard drive.

4   Select the table by single-clicking it and copy it to the clipboard (Command-C).

	2005/6	2004/5	Better/ (Worse)
Turnover	$4,822	$4,602	$220
EBITDA (per leaver)	$1,385	$1,418	($33)
Leaver costs	($37)	($8)	($29)
Depreciation and other	($692)	($704)	$12
Operating profit post leavers	656	706	(50)
Associates and other	3	(3)	6
Finance costs (net)	(100)	(154)	54
Profit before tax	599	549	50
Tax	(139)	(143)	4
Tax rate	24.9%	26.0%	1.1%
Profit for the period	420	406	14
Earning per share	5.0	4.8	0.2

5   Switch back to Keynote.

6   Select slide 7 in the slide organizer.

You're going to replace the table on the slide with the table you just selected in Pages.

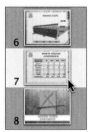

7 Select the current table on the slide and press Delete.

8 Choose Edit > Paste to add the new table.

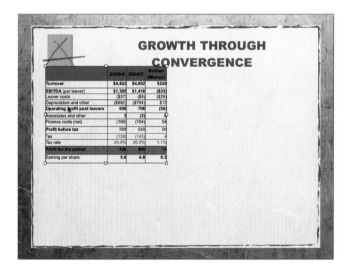

The new table needs to be sized and modified.

9 Drag the table to position it on the page. Drag the table's corners to adjust its size.

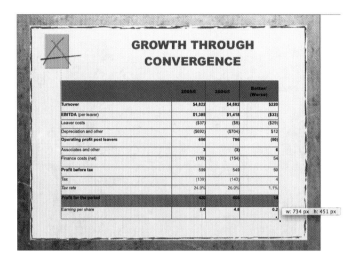

10 Select the Font panel and change the point size to 24 points.

11 Select the Slide Inspector and click Transition. Then choose the following options:

▶ Effect: 3D Effects: Swoosh

▶ Duration: 2.00 s

12 Press Command-S to save your document.

Adding Comments to a Presentation

You can add comments to a presentation that act like sticky notes. These notes can store information or to-do items related to your presentation. These notes appear while editing your slide, but are invisible when presenting the slideshow.

1   Select slide 3 in the slide organizer.

2   Click the Comment button in the toolbar to add a comment to the slide.

A virtual sticky note is added to the slide.

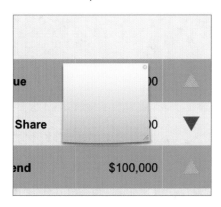

3   Click inside the note and add the following information: *Check most recent numbers in report.*

To make the note stand out even more, you can change its color

4   Select the Graphic Inspector.

5   Click the Fill color well to load the Colors window.

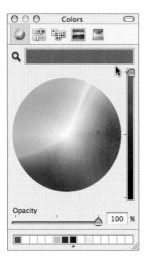

6   Choose a Red color for the note. Then close the Colors window.

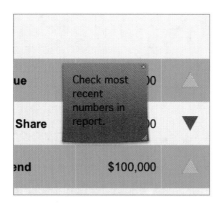

TIP If you want to permanently get rid of a note, click the X in the upper-right corner of the note.

7   Press Command-S to save your presentation.

Rehearsing the Presentation

Before giving a presentation, you'll often want to practice. This allows you to work out timing and flow issues as well as grow more comfortable with your slides. When giving your Keynote presentation, you have the option of using the presenter display. This arrangement places a timer plus speaker notes and other useful information such as the next slide all on one screen. Keynote allows you to practice your presentation and simulate the Presenter Display even without a projector hooked up.

1   Choose Keynote > Preferences to open the Preferences dialog box.

2   Click the Presenter Display icon to display the Presenter Display pane.

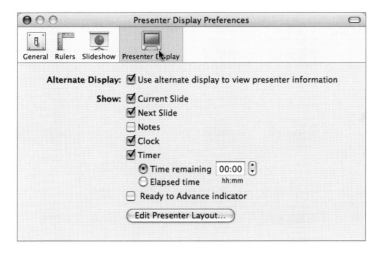

3   Enable any of the following options that you find useful:

Alternate Display: This option allows the presenter's view to show up on a laptop or second computer monitor (not the projector).

Show Current Slide: Displays the active slide.

Show Next Slide: Shows the next build or slide in the presentation.

Show Notes: Displays any speaker notes if you have added them.

Show Clock: Shows the current time of day.

Show Timer: Allows you to count down from a specific time (if you have a limit) or show how much time has passed since the start of your presentation.

Show Ready to Advance indicator: A green bar means the next build or animation is loaded and ready for playback. A red bar means you should wait before clicking.

4   Close the Preferences window.

5   Select slide 1 in the slide organizer.

6   Choose View > Rehearse Slideshow.

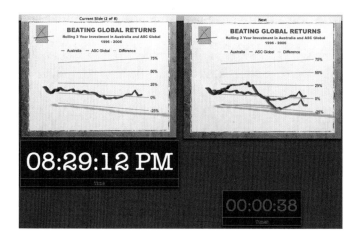

You can now rehearse your slides. You can click the spacebar to advance the presentation.

NOTE ▶ In the Presenter Display view, you cannot see animations such as transitions or builds. It is always a *very* good idea to also rehearse your slideshow by simply running it in normal mode. Choose View > Play Slideshow.

Lesson Review

1. How do you import a PowerPoint presentation into Keynote?

2. How can you convert a Microsoft Word document using the iWork suite?

3. What must you click first to add timings to a build animation?

4. How do you add comments to your presentation?

5. How do you use the presenter display to rehearse your presentation?

Answers

1. Choose File > Open; then navigate to the PowerPoint file and click Open.

2. You can launch Pages and then open a Microsoft Word document.

3. Click the More Options button to access timing controls.

4. Click the Comment button to add a virtual sticky note.

5. Choose View > Rehearse Slideshow.

5

Lesson Files

Lessons > Lesson 05 > 05Desert Starter.key

Lessons > Lesson 05 > 05Desert Theme Design.key

Lessons > Lesson 05 > 05Arizona Wildlife Final.key

Lessons > Lesson 05 > iMovie Project > Desert_
Start.iMovieProject

Lessons > Lesson 05 > Graphics

Time   This lesson takes approximately 2 hours to complete.

Goals   Create a custom theme and background

Create a photo cutout with Adobe Photoshop and Keynote

Save and share templates

Mask an image with a custom shape

Embed Web pages in a presentation

Add hyperlinks as navigation controls to a kiosk presentation

Export a presentation to CD-ROM

Working with Themes, Graphics, and Hyperlinks

While Keynote ships with several excellent templates, you may nevertheless find yourself wanting to customize or create your own. A custom theme can help a company reinforce its branding or help a teacher reinforce a presentation. A custom theme can use unique background images as well as custom fonts to improve the style of the slide.

To further enhance a presentation, Keynote supports several graphic formats. In this lesson, you'll learn how to prepare files to include transparency. You will harness Adobe Photoshop during certain parts of this lesson. If you do not own this program, you have two options. The first is to download a 30-day trial from Adobe's Web site. The second option is to read the steps using Photoshop, but then use the prepared images that can be found in the Lesson 05 folder.

You will build an interactive presentation with navigation during this exercise.

You will also see how to add Web views and Web links to a presentation to capture frequently updated information. For example, you could embed a Web page that shows changing interest rates into a presentation. You'll also learn how to incorporate hyperlinks to navigate between slides, which is very useful if the presentation is being run on a kiosk. Finally, you'll save your presentation to a CD-ROM.

Creating a Custom Theme

Customizing a theme can be a bit intimidating at first as there are lots of options to modify and components to work with. However, the end result is very rewarding and can be a big time-saver for future projects. This lesson will show you the essential steps needed, but a few steps are done for you to conserve time. Additionally, we will just touch the surface when working with Adobe Photoshop. This powerful image editing application is used for advanced graphics work and is an industry standard. To learn more, consider picking up *Understanding Adobe Photoshop: Digital Imaging Concepts and Techniques*, also published by Peachpit Press.

Creating an Empty Theme

There is no such thing as a completely blank page in a Keynote. This is because you must choose a theme to work with from the Theme Chooser when you launch the application or choose File > New. To make creating your custom theme easier, you'll create a starter file based on the White theme.

1   Launch Keynote or, if Keynote is already open, choose File > New to access the Theme Chooser.

2   Choose the White theme and set the size to 1024 × 768; then click Choose.

A new document based on the theme is created.

3   Choose View > Show Master Slides to see the master slides for this theme.

Master slides contain all of the layout options for a slide that can be used in a presentation.

4   Expand the master slides organizer to see more of the slide masters by
dragging the resize handle downward.

You are going to remove several masters from the theme to simplify it.

5   Select the Title & Bullets – 2 Column master and press Delete.

6   Repeat the selection and deletion commands for the following master
slide types:

▶   Title – Top

▶   Title – Center

▶   Photo – Horizontal

▶   Photo – Horizontal Reflection

▶   Photo – Vertical Reflection

▶   Title, Bullets & Photo

▶   Title & Bullets – Left

▶   Title & Bullets – Right

7   Choose File > Save and save the presentation to your hard drive. Name it
Theme Starter.

Creating a Title Page

It is a good idea to have a title page for each section of your presentation. This helps your audience better follow the presentation and signifies when the presentation is addressing a new topic. The slide theme that you are working on is for a presentation about the Arizona desert. The slide design will match the subject matter.

1   In the Master Slides area, select the Title & Subtitle slide. Then select the text in the Title Text block.

2   Press Command-T to open the Font panel. Then set the font to Hoefler Text, Black, 96 pt.

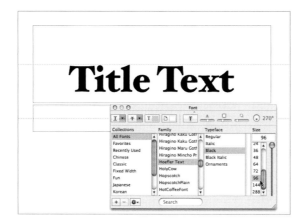

3   Select all of the text in the block that begins "Body Level One" and change the font to Hoefler Text, Regular, 36 pt.

You'll now add a photo to serve as the background of the slide.

4   Click the Inspector button to open the inspector; then choose the Master Slide Inspector and click Appearance.

5   From the Background pop-up menu, choose Image Fill.

An Open dialog box asks you to select a file.

6   Navigate to the Lesson 05 folder, open the Graphics folder and then the Backgrounds folder, choose the file **Background 1.jpg**, and click Open.

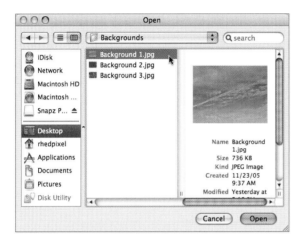

The image appears behind the title text. You need to tweak the text to improve its readability.

7   Click the Title Text box; then hold down the Shift key and click Body Level One to add this text to the selection.

8   In the toolbar, click the Colors button to open the Colors window; then click a white color swatch at the bottom of the palette and drag it onto the first text box. Drag another white swatch onto the second.

Now you'll add a shadow to the text to add edge contrast.

9 Open the Graphics Inspector and select the Shadow check box to add a shadow to the text. The default values are fine.

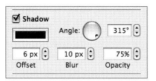

10 In the toolbar, click the Shapes button and add a rectangle.

This rectangle will serve as a banner behind the slide title. The rectangle has an image fill (the default in the White theme we used as our model), but we want a plain black fill.

11 In the Graphics Inspector, choose Color Fill from the Fill menu and click the color well to change the fill color to black. Set the opacity to 50%. Then size the rectangle to be slightly taller then the text and to extend from edge to edge on the slide.

12 Choose Arrange > Send to Back.

13 Choose File > Save As and save the file as *Desert Theme Design* in your Lesson 05 folder.

Creating a Background and Formatting Text

Now you will create a custom background for the bullets pages. To do this, you will use photos plus the Adjust Image window and Graphic Inspector.

1   In the Master Slides area, select the Title & Bullets master.

2   Select the Master Slide Inspector and make sure Appearance is selected.

3   Click the Background color well to open the Colors window. Click the Crayon button to view preset colors and choose Cantaloupe from the bottom row.

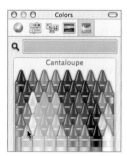

4   Choose Insert > Choose and navigate to the Lesson 05 folder, open the Graphics folder, open the Backgrounds folder, and choose **Background 2.jpg**; then click Insert.

The image is added to the front of the slide, obscuring the text.

5   In the toolbar, click the Adjust button to open the Adjust Image window. Then drag the Saturation slider all the way to the left and adjust the Temperature slider to 20.

The image is now desaturated with a slight color tint.

6   Close the Adjust Image window.

7   In the Graphic Inspector, lower the Opacity to 30% to blend the texture with the colored background.

The photo needs to be sent to the back so that it does not interfere with the text.

8   Choose Arrange > Send to Back.

Now you will adjust the fonts on the canvas.

9   Select the Title Text block of text and press Command-T to open the Font panel. Set the font to Hoefler Text, Black, 72 pt.

10   Select the text block containing the bullet points and change the font to Hoefler Text, Black, 36 pt.

11   Click the Title Text box, and then hold down the Shift key and click Body Level One to add it to the selection.

12   In the toolbar, click the Colors button to open the Colors palette; then click a white color swatch at the bottom of the palette and drag it onto the first text box and then drag again onto the second.

13   Open the Graphics Inspector and select the Shadow check box to add a shadow to the text. Set the following values:

▶   Offset: 5 px (the distance)

▶ Blur: 5 px (the softness)

▶ Opacity: 75%

14 Switch to the Text Inspector and make sure the Text button is active.

15 Select the Body bullets text box and click the Align to Top button.

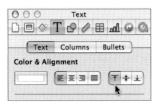

You now need to apply the same formatting to the next master slide, called Bullets.

16 Select the photo on the current slide, choose Edit > Copy.

17 Switch to the Bullets master slide and choose Edit > Paste; then choose Arrange > Send to Back.

18 Select the Master Slide Inspector and make sure the Appearance area is active. Change the background color fill to Cantaloupe.

19 Switch back to the Title & Bullets slide; then double-click the Body Level One text and choose Format > Copy Style.

20 Switch back to the Bullets slide and double-click the text block and press Command-A to select all of the text.

21 Choose Format > Paste Style to change the text attributes to match.

22 Select the Blank master slide.

23 Select the Master Slide Inspector and choose Image Fill from the Background pop-up menu. Then click Choose.

The Backgrounds folder opens as it was last selected.

24 Choose **Background 3.jpg** and click Insert.

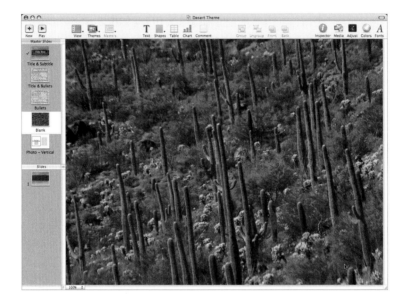

You now need to switch programs to build more slide masters.

25 Choose File > Save to save your work in progress.

Creating a Photo Cutout with Photoshop and Keynote

Among the most popular features of Keynote are the photo cutout slides. These are slides with openings where you can drop photos.

When you're creating your own theme, you may want to create a photo cutout as well. You can create your own photo cutouts using Adobe Photoshop and Keynote. You will build a photo cutout from scratch using Photoshop. If you do not have Photoshop, you can use the **Photo Cutout.png** file to create the master slide.

Preparing the Photoshop File

Advanced graphics professionals frequently use Adobe Photoshop to process multi-layered graphic images. For your custom theme, you will create a photo cutout with a box to hold the image and a drop shadow and stroke to offset the box.

1   Open Adobe Photoshop by clicking its icon in the Dock or locating it in your Applications folder.

    If you don't have Photoshop, you can just read along and learn the process or skip to step 20.

2   Choose File > Open and navigate to the Lesson 05 folder. Open the Graphics folder and then the PSD files folder; choose the file **Cutout Start.psd**.

This file has two layers: a sandy-textured layer and a layer containing a white box surrounded by transparency. The white box represents the area that will be cut out of the photo cutout. You will use this file to create a photo cutout for Keynote.

3   Choose Window > Workspace > Reset Palette Locations to restore the Photoshop interface to its default configuration.

4   In the Layers palette, click the layer named Box.

You are going to use the Layer Effects feature to add a beveled edge and drop shadow to the Box layer. Taken together, those layer effects constitute a layer style.

5   Click the small *f* in a circle at the bottom of the Layers palette to access the Layer Effects. From the menu, choose Drop Shadow.

The Layer Style dialog box opens .

6   Set the Drop Shadow options to match the following figure.

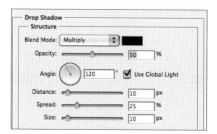

You will now add a stroke to the edge of the box to increase contrast.

7   In the Styles list, click the word "Stroke" to add a stroke to the layer and to choose options for the stroke.

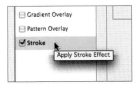

8   Set the Stroke options to match the following figure.

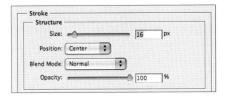

These settings add a thick stroke centered around the outside edge.

9   Click the color well to open the Adobe Color picker (it is similar to the one found in iWork). Enter the following RGB values to pick a brown color:

▶   R: 182

▶   G: 124

▶   B: 13

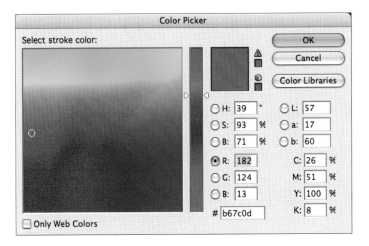

10 Click OK to close the Color Picker. The stroke can be beveled to improve its appearance.

11 In the Styles list, click the words Bevel and Emboss to apply a bevel to the edge of the Box layer. Set the Bevel and Emboss options to match the following figure.

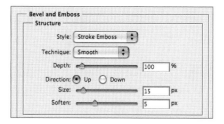

12 Click OK to apply the layer style.

The white area of the box needs to be transparent so the photo can show through.

13 With the Box layer still selected, set the Fill opacity slider to 0% to reduce the opacity of the original layer without affecting the layer effects that you have applied.

You now need to create a hole in the Sand layer so you can see through it. This is where the photo will be placed in Keynote.

14 Hold down the Command key and click the Box layer thumbnail in the Layers palette to create a selection the same size and shape as the layer. This selection can be used to create a hole.

15 Select the Sand layer by clicking its thumbnail in the Layers palette. Then press Delete.

The part of the Sand layer enclosed in the selection is removed, creating a hole. A grid of gray squares will show through, indicating transparency.

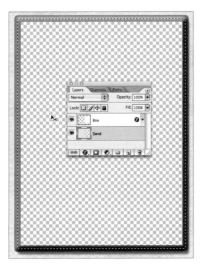

The file now needs to be saved in the PNG format so you can import it into Keynote.

16   Choose File > Save As. In the Save dialog box, name the file **Photo Cutout Final**; then in the Format menu, choose PNG.

17   Click Save; leave the PNG Interlace options set to None and click OK to create the file.

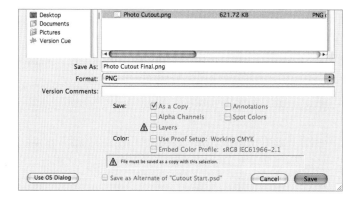

You should now save your layered PSD file in case you need to make future changes in Photoshop.

18   Choose File > Save As, name the file **Photo Cutout.psd**, and click Save.

19   Close the open document.

Leave Photoshop open; you will return to it for a few more tasks in a moment.

20   Switch back to Keynote.

Building the Keynote Slide Master

Now that the photo cutout is saved as a PNG file, it can be placed into Keynote. This will create a page that can hold photos and text.

1   In the slide organizer, select the Photo – Vertical master slide.

2   Click the background image in the canvas.

The image does not appear to be selected, but this is because it is locked (look closely at the corners of the image). A locked image cannot be modified or moved—a good choice for a master slide.

3   Choose Arrange > Unlock. Then press Delete to remove the existing photo cutout.

4   Choose Insert > Choose and navigate to the PSD Files folder in your Lesson 05 folder and then to the cutout file. Select the file **Photo Cutout Final.png** that you created in Photoshop.

TIP ▶ If you skipped the Photoshop steps, you can use the file **Photo Cutout.png**.

5   Click Insert to add the graphic.

The graphic is added to your slide, but it obscures the text.

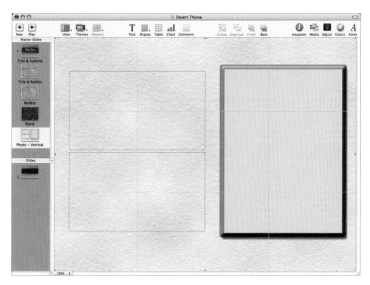

6 Choose Arrange > Send to Back to move the cutout to the bottom of the image stack.

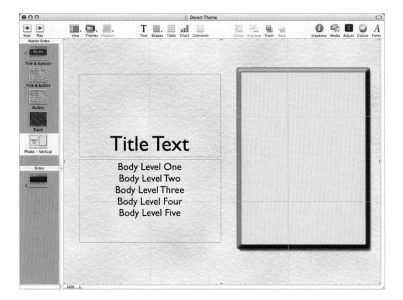

The photo cutout needs to be locked and formatted to work properly.

7 Choose Arrange > Lock to protect the cutout from accidental modification.

8 Open the Master Slide Inspector and click Appearance. Ensure that the "Allow objects on slide to layer with master" check box is selected.

This setting allows you to layer imported photos with the photo cutout.

Now the text on the slide needs to be formatted to match the rest of your slides.

9 Select the Title Text block and open the Font panel. Change the font to Hoefler Text, Black, 54 pt.

The body text needs to be formatted for the description of the photo.

10 Select the body text; then change the font to Hoefler Text, Regular, 28 pt. When you're done, close the Font panel.

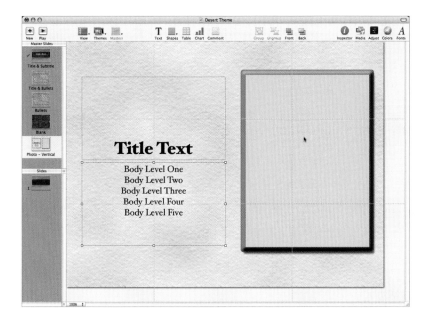

Now the text boxes need to be formatted and resized. Your photos will have long descriptions, so you need to make the title box smaller and the body text block larger.

11 Select the Title Text block. Grab the bottom edge and drag upward to resize the block to a height of 175 px.

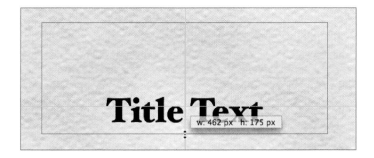

12 Select the Body Level text block and open the Text Inspector. Click the alignment button to left-justify the text in the text block.

13 Grab the top edge and drag upward to resize the block to a height of 350 px.

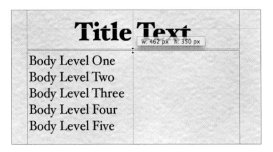

The formatting is now complete.

14 Choose File > Save to save your work so far.

Saving and Sharing Themes

While building our custom theme so far, we have been saving it as a presentation file. You can save the modifications you have made as a new custom theme. Saving a theme allows you to apply the formatting to another existing presentation or create an entirely new presentation based on your custom theme. The theme you have been working on so far is ready to be saved as a custom theme.

1 With the file 05Desert Theme Design open, choose File > Save Theme.

A sheet opens with the default Themes folder selected to store custom themes.

2 Name your theme *Desert Theme*. Then click Save to save the theme.

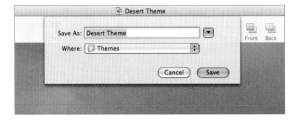

The theme file is written to your Themes folder and will appear in the Theme Chooser when you launch the program or activate the Theme Chooser.

It's a good idea to duplicate the custom theme to back it up or share with other users.

3   Follow this path to find your custom theme: Macintosh HD > Users > (User folder) > Library > Application Support > iWork > Keynote > Themes.

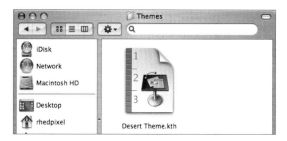

You'll back up your Keynote theme file by copying it to your Documents folder.

4   Select the file **Desert Theme.kth**; then hold down the Option key and drag the file to the Documents folder shortcut in the Themes window. When a plus symbol appears, release the mouse to copy the file.

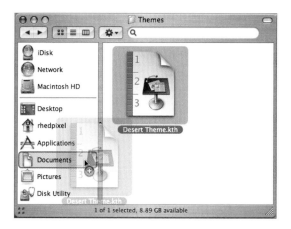

The file is now backed up. You can also share it with other users.

5   Close the Desert Theme Design file.

Applying a Custom Theme

The theme file is prepped and can now be applied to an existing presentation. The text content for this exercise has already been entered on slides. However, the slides are generic and need styling and images.

1   Choose File > Open, navigate to the Lesson 05 folder, and open the file **05Desert Starter.key**.

2   Choose File > Save As and rename the presentation *Arizona Wildlife* and save it in your Lesson 05 folder.

You can now apply a theme to the presentation.

3   Choose File > Choose Theme to open the Theme Chooser. Select Desert Theme and click Choose.

Custom themes appear at the bottom of the Theme Chooser.

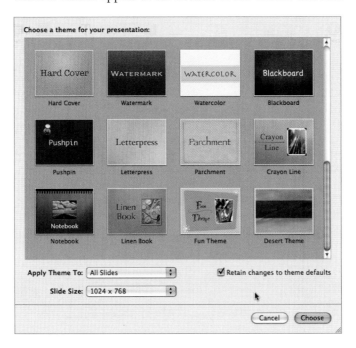

The Desert Theme custom theme is applied to your presentation. Because the slide masters of both presentations used the same names (Bullets… Blank), the program matches the new formatting to the appropriate slide.

A few items need to be forced to properly format themselves as not all fonts and point sizes changed to match the new theme.

4 Click Slide 1 in the slide organizer, choose Edit > Select All to select all slides, and choose Format > Reapply Master to Slide.

The slides now completely match the template. You can now customize the slides to complete the presentation.

5 Select slide 4 in the slide organizer (Arizona Mountain Lion).

6 In the Finder, navigate to the Lesson 05 folder and open the Animals folder. Drag the file **arizona mountain lion.JPG** into the photo cutout.

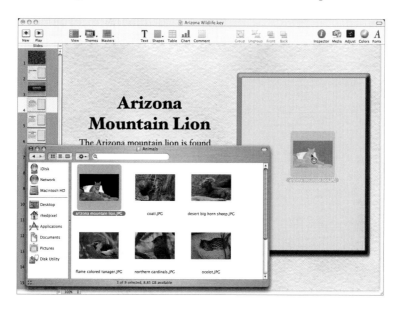

You can drag the photo in the canvas if you need to reposition it.

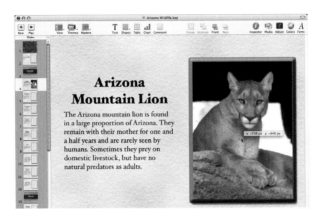

7 Drag in the photos for slides 5 to 12 using the photos in the Animals folder. Reposition or resize photos to taste and use the Adjust Image window if needed.

> **TIP** ▸ You can use the Metrics Inspector to precisely size or flip an image if needed.

8 In the slide organizer, select slide 14 (Chain Fruit Cholla).

Now you're going to build the next section of the presentation.

9 In the Finder, navigate to the Lesson 05 folder, open the Plants folder, and drag the file **Chain Fruit Cholla.JPG** into the photo cutout.

10 Select slide 15 in the slide organizer.

The title for the plant is partially cut off, so you must resize the text block to make it fit.

11 Click the Hedge Cactus text block to select it. Hold down the Option key and drag the right edge of the text block to make the text block wider (the block scales in both directions).

12 Add the remaining plant photos to slides 15 to 20.

Size and position the photos to taste and make any adjustments you feel are needed.

13 Select slide 22 and select the title text (it is cut off, as evidenced by the plus symbol at the bottom of the text block). Press Command- – (minus) to reduce the font size 1 point at a time. Repeat until the text fits.

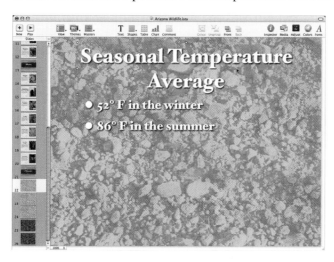

14 Repeat the formatting for the next two slides.

The presentation is not complete, but you need to switch to Photoshop, iMovie, and Safari to finish preparing content.

15 Choose File > Save to save your work in progress.

Adding Transparency to Artwork

For your presentation, you will create four graphics that can be added to the Keynote presentation: a piece of clip art to be used on slides and three navigation symbols that you will use to control movement between slides.

You need to add some artwork to your slides, but you don't want the entire image to show up as a rectangular block. Finding artwork with transparency built-in is uncommon. You can purchase specialty file collections on CD or DVD or purchase files online, or if you are a little bit Photoshop savvy, you can create your own.

Just as before, if you do not have access to Photoshop you can read through the Photoshop steps and use the completed file **Cactus.psd**.

1 Switch to Adobe Photoshop.

> **TIP** ▶ You'll want to make Photoshop more compatible with Keynote by opening Photoshop > Preferences > File Handling. In the File Compatibility area, open the Maximize PSD and PSB File Compatibility menu and choose Always. Then close the Preferences window.

2 Choose File > Open and navigate to the Lesson 05 folder, open the Graphics folder and then the Clip Art folder, and select **Cactus.JPG**; click Open.

JPEG files do not contain transparency information. To use transparency, you must convert the *Background* image into a layer.

3   Double-click Background. In the dialog box that opens, name the layer
Cactus; then click OK.

You now need to select and delete the sky.

4   Choose Select > Color Range to make a selection based on color. Click an
area near the cactus to select a shade of blue.

The black-and-white image in the dialog box represents the selection
you are creating. White is selected, black is not selected, and gray is partially selected. You need to select more of the sky if you want to remove
all of it.

5   Hold down the Shift key and drag through more of the sky to add more
shades of blue to the selection. Drag until the sky is selected. You can also
adjust the Fuzziness slider to soften the selection and have a gentler edge
around the cactus.

6   Click OK to create the selection.

The sky is selected and can now be removed. Instead of deleting it, you will use a better technique called layer masking, which is easier to modify.

7   Choose Layer > Layer Mask > Hide Selection.

A layer mask is added to the image, hiding the sky—Photoshop's transparency grid is visible.

There is a slight blue fringe at the edge of the cactus where the sky and spines mix. You need to get rid of this.

8   Click the layer mask thumbnail in the Layers palette (the black-and-white icon next to the layer thumbnail).

9   Choose Image > Adjustments > Levels to apply a Levels adjustment.

This adjustment is similar to the those that you have made in the Adjust Image window in iWork.

In the layer mask, the boundary between the white and black areas is not a sharp line, but a region containing shades of gray, This gray area in the mask lets some of the blue sky show through and corresponds to much of the blue fringe we see.

10 Move the middle (gray) slider to the right to darken the grays in the mask. Then click OK.

This tightens up the edge of the cactus and removes most of the blue fringe.

11 Choose File > Save and save the file in its default location. Name the file *Cactus Final*.

Because the JPG format does not support either layers or transparency, Photoshop changes the file's format to PSD (the native Photoshop file format). The transparency information in a PSD file is also recognized by Keynote.

12 Close the open document.

There are three more pieces you need to prep for your Keynote presentation.

13 Choose File > Open and navigate to the Lesson 05 folder; then choose the
Graphics folder and then the PSD Files folder and open the file **Navigation
Small.psd**.

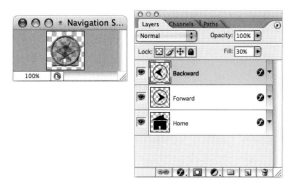

This file contains all three navigation symbols on separate layers in one document. They need to be split up into separate documents (one per button).

14 Choose File > Scripts > Export Layers To Files.

A dialog box opens asking you to set destination and naming information.

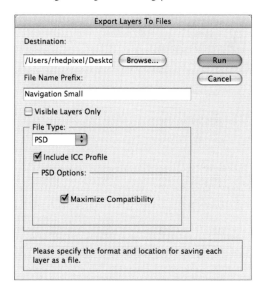

15 Click the Browse button and navigate to the PSD files folder (it should be selected by default).

16 Make the File Name Prefix box blank. In the File Type menu, choose PSD and make sure that Maximize Compatibility is selected.

17 Click Run to create the three separate files. When a dialog box opens telling you that the export to layers was successful, click OK.

You are now done with Adobe Photoshop for this lesson.

18 Quit Photoshop.

19 Switch back to Keynote and select slide 3 in the slide organizer.

20 Choose Insert > Choose, navigate to the Lesson 05 folder, open the Graphics folder, open the Clip Art folder, and choose the file Cactus Final.psd; then click Insert.

21 The cactus is too large, so in the Metrics Inspector, enter a height of 500 px.

22 Position the cactus in the lower-right corner of the slide.

23 Choose Edit > Copy. Switch to slide 13 and choose Edit > Paste. Then switch to slide 21 and choose Edit > Paste again.

24 Choose File > Save to save your work in progress.

Masking Photos with Shapes

You can use shapes to create containers for your image. You can use this technique to crop a photo to a non-square shape, opening up new design possibilities for your slides. Here, you'll place images within a circle.

1 Working in the same presentation as in the preceding exercise, select slide 22 in the slide organizer.

2 In the toolbar, click the Shapes button and select a circle to add to your presentation.

3 Set an equal height and width of 350 px for the circle and place the shape in the lower-right corner of the slide.

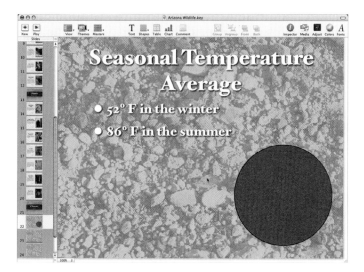

4 Open the Graphics Inspector and add a drop shadow to the circle.

The default values are fine for the shadow.

5 With the circle selected, choose Edit > Copy.

6 Switch to the next slide and choose Edit > Paste. Repeat the paste operation on slide 24.

7 Switch back to slide 22 by clicking its thumbnail in the slide organizer.

8 Choose Insert > Choose to add a photo to the slide. Navigate to the Lesson 05 folder, open the Graphics folder and then Climate folder, and choose **Climate 1.JPG**; then click Choose.

The photo is added to the slide.

9 Hold down the Shift key and click the blue circle to add it to the selection.

10 Choose Format > Mask with Shape to use the circle as a mask.

The mask is applied, but the image needs to be repositioned.

11 Drag the image down and to the right to reposition it within the circle. Double-click the image to apply the mask.

The shadow is no longer present since the shape was used as a mask, so it must be added again.

12 In the Graphic Inspector, select Shadow to enable it. Then choose a solid line from the Stroke pop-up menu and set the thickness field to 4 px to apply a stroke to the masked photo to make the photo stand out more.

13 Switch to the next slide and add and format **Climate 2.JPG** using the same
techniques as you just used. Then do the same for **Climate 3.JPG**.

14 On slide 24, click to place the insertion point before the words *(summer
and winter)*. Then press Option-Return to wrap the text to a new line
without creating a new bullet.

15 Choose File > Save to save your work in progress.

Embedding a Web Page

Sometimes in a presentation, you will want a snapshot of a Web page. This can
be used as a link to a Web page, or just as slide content that can be updated
automatically when connected to the Internet. For the purpose of this presentation, which will run in a self-guided mode called kiosk view, you want the
Web view as content only and not as a link.

1 Select slide 25 in the slide organizer.

2 Choose Insert > Web View and in the Hyperlink Inspector select the
Enable as a hyperlink check box.

3 Enter the following Web address in the URL field: *http://www.wrh. noaa.gov/twc/*.

This is a link to a page with current weather information for the Sonoran Desert area in Arizona.

The Web view is added to the page but needs to be resized.

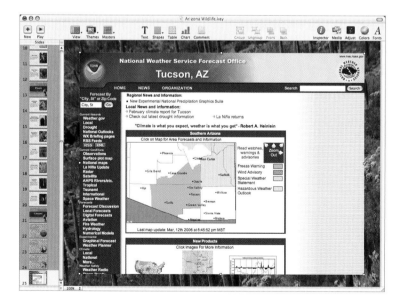

4   Drag the bottom edge of the Web view toward the bottom of the slide.

We now need to offset the Web view for readability. A drop shadow can help.

5   Enable the drop shadow in the Graphics Inspector and set the offset and blur values to 10 px.

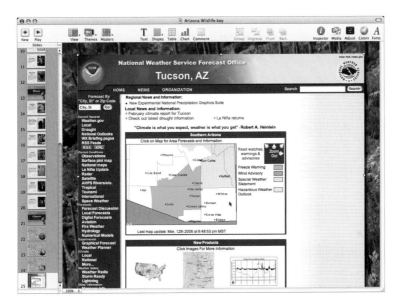

6   Choose File > Save to save your work in progress.

Embedding and Formatting QuickTime Movies

Full-motion video is a popular feature in interactive presentations. However, you must process the video file to optimize its appearance in Keynote. To modify the QuickTime file, you must have QuickTime Pro installed. If you own any of the Apple professional video applications, QuickTime Pro is unlocked; otherwise, you can purchase QuickTime Pro from Apple's Web site for a small charge.

NOTE ▶ If you want extra practice editing in iMovie, you can open the file **Desert_Start.iMovieProject** in the iMovie Project folder. This iMovie project contains several shots of the Arizona desert. Additionally, you can examine or modify the audio score by opening the file **Desert.band** in the Music folder.

1   Open QuickTime Player by clicking its icon in the Dock.

2   Choose File > Open, navigate to the Lesson 05 folder, choose iMovie Project > Desert_Start.iMovieProject > Shared Movies > iDvd > **desert.mov**, and click OK.

3   Click the Play button at the bottom of the screen and watch the movie.

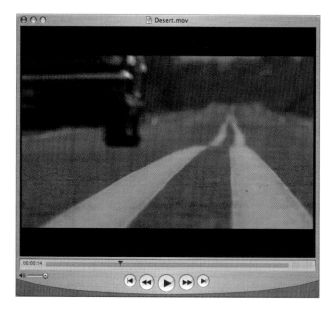

4　Press Command-J to open the movie properties for the file.

5　Click to select the Video Track and then click the Visual Settings button.

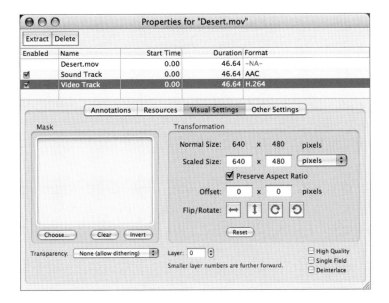

6　For Scaled Size, specify 1024 × 768 so the video fills the slide, and select the High Quality check box for maximum playback quality.

7　Save and then close the movie file. Quit QuickTime Player.

8　In Keynote, select slide 1 in the slide organizer.

9　Choose Insert > Choose, navigate to the Lesson 05 folder, select the file **Desert.mov**, and click Choose.

　　The movie file is large enough to fill the entire slide.

10　Open the Slide Inspector and click Transition. Choose the following options for the slide transition:

　　▶　Effect: 2D Effects: Fade Through Color

　　▶　Duration: 2.00 s

▶ Start Transition: Automatically

▶ Delay: 47.0 s (the movie is 47 seconds long, so the transition will occur when the movie finishes playing).

11 Choose File > Save to save your work in progress.

The introductory video is added to slide 1 and embedded in the Keynote file. You can now add navigation controls to the slides.

Adding Hyperlinks and Navigation

Keynote allows you to add controls to navigate between slides. In some cases, you will want the user to be able to navigate through the presentation using Hyperlinks in a self-guided manner (and not necessarily in linear order).

1 Open the Document Inspector and click Document to see properties for the presentation.

2 Change the presentation mode to Hyperlinks only.

3   Select slide 2 in the slide organizer.

This slide needs a little more formatting and to have links added.

4   In the Finder, open the Lesson 05 folder and drag the file **Menu Title.JPG** into the photo cutout on slide 2. Size and position the photo to taste.

5   Select the lower text block with the three menu choices (Animals, Plants, and Climate).

6 Select the Text Inspector and click the Bullets button. Change the Bullet options to match the following figure:

7 Select both text blocks on the page. Press Command- = (equals sign) to increase the point size 1 point per click. Make the text approximately 30 percent larger so it matches the following figure (approximately 15 clicks).

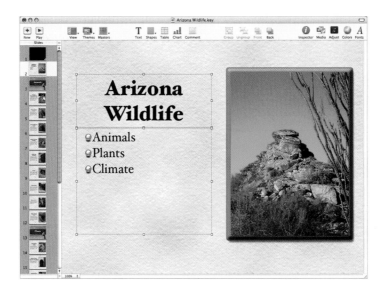

8 Double-click the word *Animals* to select it individually.

9   In the Hyperlink Inspector, select the Enable as a hyperlink check box; choose Slide from the Link To menu and then select the Slide button and choose 3 from the menu (the Animals slide in the slide organizer).

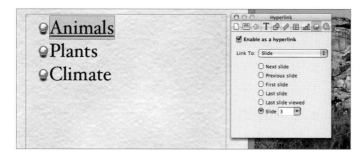

10 As you did for Animals, link Plants to slide 13 and Climate to slide 21.

You now have links from the main menu page to each section; now you need to add links for all of the body pages for navigation.

11 Select slide 3 in the slide organizer.

12 Switch to the Finder and open the Lesson 05 folder; then open the PSD Files folder. Find the files that you created by exporting layers from the **Navigation Small.psd** file in Photoshop (their names will include "Backward," "Forward," and "Home." Select these files by Shift-clicking them.

13 Drag the files to the middle of the slide canvas in slide 3 and release.

The navigation symbols are added to your canvas.

14 Drag the navigation symbols to the lower-left corner of the canvas and arrange them to match the following figure.

15 Select the left-pointing arrow (the Back symbol) and open the Hyperlink Inspector.

16 Select the Enable as a hyperlink check box; for Link To, choose Slide and then choose Previous slide.

17 Select the right-pointing arrow (the Forward symbol) and set the hyperlink to Next slide.

18 Select the Home symbol and set the hyperlink to Slide 2 (the menu you designed earlier).

19 Shift-click to select all three navigation symbols and then choose Edit > Copy. Select each slide (4 to 25) in turn and paste the hyperlinks into each.

> **TIP** ▶ You can click a slide's thumbnail in the slide organizer to switch slides and then press Command-V to paste the Clipboard contents (the navigation buttons).

20 On slide 25, delete the Forward symbol (there are no more slides to advance to).

21 Select slide 25 in the slide organizer; then hold down the Shift key and click slide 2 to select slides 2 to 25.

22 In the Slide Inspector, click Transition and set the Effect to 3D Effects: Cube.

23 Choose File > Save to save your work in progress.

Running a Presentation in Kiosk Mode

The presentation is just about completed. You need to make just a few modifications to control the presentation playback experience. Kiosk-style presentations are meant to be run from a computer without supervision. They are often deployed in museums and retail environments.

1 Open the Document Inspector and click the Document button.

2 Select "Restart show if idle" and set the time to 5 m (minutes).

3 If you want, select "Require password to exit show."

> **NOTE ▶** If you choose this option, you *must* know your username and password to exit. If you do not, you'll have to power down the computer and reboot.

4 Choose Keynote > Preferences and click the General button. In the Saving area of the dialog, ensure that both the "Copy audio and movies into document" and "Copy theme images into document" check boxes are selected.

This option stores all of the required resources (other than fonts) in the project file so it will work on another computer.

5 Close the Preferences window.

6 Choose File > Save to save your presentation.

7 Click the Play button to view your presentation. When you are done exploring, press the Esc key (if you have chosen to require a password, you must enter the username and password for the computer you are on).

Your presentation is complete and ready for playback on any system running Keynote.

You can compare your completed project to **05 Arizona Wildlife Final.key** in the Lesson 05 folder.

Exporting to CD-ROM

Ideally, you would play back the interactive presentation using Keynote. Remember, you can install the 30-day trial copy of Keynote on any qualifying Mac and it will continue to function as a player that allows you to view files even after the 30-day period is up.

You can export your presentation to a CD-ROM—useful if you need it to run on a Windows computer (with QuickTime installed) or on a Mac without iWork installed.

1   Select slide 1 and open the Slide Inspector and remove the delay from the transition.

Leaving the delay in will add a large amount of black after the movie. While you need this timing for kiosk mode, it interferes when exporting a QuickTime movie.

2   Choose File > Export. Then select QuickTime and set the options to match the following figure:

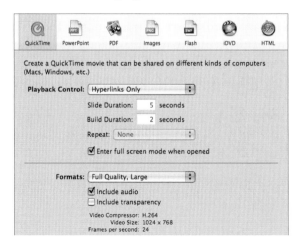

3 Click Next and then name the file and set a destination such as your desktop. Click Export.

Depending on the speed of your computer, it may take several minutes to export the file.

4 When the export is finished, open the QuickTime movie to test it.

All of the Navigation controls and transitions should work fine. Image quality won't be as good as in Keynote, but it should still be pretty clean.

5 Burn the QuickTime movie to a CD-ROM for playback on another machine.

Lesson Review

1. Name two graphic formats that can be imported into Keynote and keep their transparency intact.

2. How can you view master slides?

3. How can you add a Web page into your presentation?

4. How do you set a presentation to advance slides only by clicking hyperlinks?

5. How can you create a button to advance one slide?

Answers

1. You can use PSD files or PNG files.

2. Choose View > Show Master Slides to see their thumbnails in the slide organizer.

3. Choose Insert > Web View to add a graphic representing the Web page. You can set it to update automatically or enable it as a hyperlink.

4. In the Document Inspector, click Document and then click the Presentation pop-up menu and change it to Hyperlinks only.

5. Add a graphic to a slide; then, in the Hyperlink Inspector, select the Enable as a hyperlink check box. Specify that you want to link to a slide and then choose the Next slide option.

6

Lesson Files Lessons > Lesson 06 > 06Photo Portfolio.key

Lessons > Lesson 06 > 06Portfolio_Start.band

Lessons > Lesson 06 > Portfolio Samples

Time This lesson takes approximately 90 minutes to complete.

Goals Print speaker notes and handouts

Export a QuickTime movie

Export a PowerPoint presentation

Export to PDF

Export images for use in other applications

Export an interactive Flash file

Send a project to iDVD

Export to HTML for the Internet

Create a podcast using GarageBand

Give a presentation with a laptop

Lesson 6

Publishing and Giving Your Presentation

When you complete a presentation, you'll want to get it out into the world. Keynote has several export modules that allow you to publish your presentation. The concept is essentially "create once, publish many." By allowing you to export to a DVD, a PDF file, the Internet, and even your iPod, Keynote ensures that your good ideas and important information can be seen by a large audience.

To practice the various output techniques, you'll use an existing presentation. It harnesses the flexible Modern Portfolio template to showcase some photography. You can use this template to create your own portfolio to show to prospective clients.

As you'll see in this lesson, you can export a completed slideshow to a variety of formats.

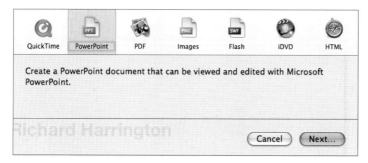

Keynote supports many export formats to help you to share your presentation.

Adding and Printing Speaker Notes

You can include speaker notes—which Keynote calls presenter notes—with your Keynote presentation to prompt you as you give the presentation. You can add speaker notes to each slide and then view them on an alternate display during your presentation; the audience won't be able to see your notes.

> **TIP** ▶ Choose View > Show Presenter Notes to see notes for a presentation. Click in the field below the canvas to add speaker notes.

1 Open the Keynote presentation for which you want to print speaker notes. For this task, you can open the file **06Photo Portfolio.key** in the Lesson folder.

2 Add the following text to slide 4:

Discuss using Adjust window to create Black & White photos within Keynote.

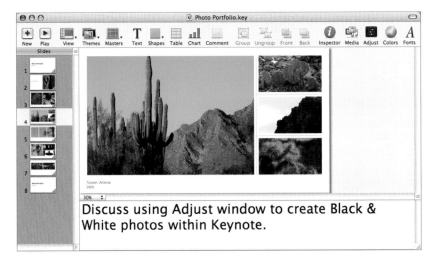

3 Choose File > Print; then from the pop-up menu below the Presets menu, choose Keynote.

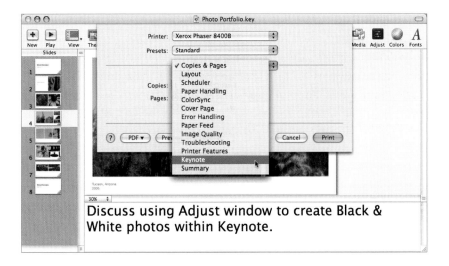

4   In the Print options, select Slides With Notes.

This option prints a single slide per page with your speaker notes below.

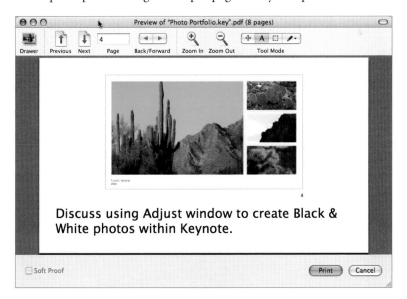

TIP To print multiple slides per page with notes, select the Handout option.

5 Use the menu below the Presets menu to select other printer options such as the number of copies and print quality; then click Print.

Printing Handouts

Oftentimes you'll want to hand out your speaker notes to those attending a speech or meeting. These notes can be a great takeaway for your audience and will help them review the information you are presenting.

> **TIP ▶** Many speakers give out their handouts after their speeches. This way, audience members won't skip ahead in the presentation or spend the whole time reading the notes.

1 With the presentation for which you want to print handouts open, choose File > Print (Command-P).

Here, we're using **06Photo Portfolio.key**.

2 In the menu below the Presets menu, choose Keynote.

3 In the Print options, select Handout.

This option prints multiple slides per page as well as other user-specified information.

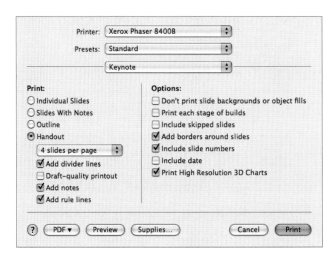

TIP ▸ Want a simpler handout? Select Outline and just print your outline instead. This will create a text-only version of your presentation.

4 Use the pop-up menu under the Presets menu to access and adjust other printer options such as the number of copies and print quality, and then click Print.

TIP ▸ To see what your printed pages will look like without using any actual paper, click Preview in the Print dialog box. Keynote will generate a temporary PDF file from your document and display it in the Preview application. If you like what you see, click the Print button in the lower-right corner of the Preview window. If what you see is not what you were expecting, click Cancel.

TIP ▸ To save printing costs (and speed up printing), use the Draft-quality printout option.

Exporting to QuickTime

In Lessons 3 and 5, we explored Keynote's robust support for QuickTime media import and playback. The output options in Keynote are just as powerful. We'll take a quick tour here that will suit many reader's needs. For those who want more, see Lesson 11, "For the Power User."

1   With the file you want to export open, choose File > Export.

Here, we're still using **06Photo Portfolio.key**.

The Export dialog box opens with several options.

2   Click the QuickTime button to access movie options.

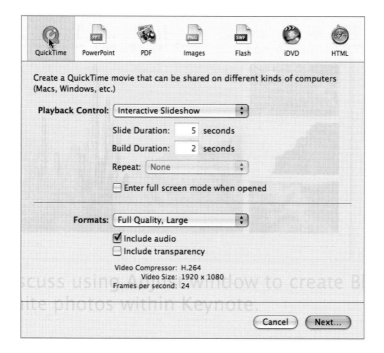

Your choices in the QuickTime options depend on the purpose of your QuickTime movie. For example, do you want to make a movie that runs interactively on a desktop computer, or are you trying to convert your presentation so you can edit it together with video in iMovie?

3   Choose a Playback Control method:

▶   Interactive Slideshow: This option gives viewers total control over the slideshow as they can click to advance slides. This is a good option for self-paced learning or as a backup of your presentation.

▶   Hyperlinks Only: This option lets the presentation run in Kiosk mode. The user can only click buttons or links to navigate to other slides or Web pages.

▶   Self-Playing Movie: This option runs the slideshow with no user interaction. You must set slide duration and build options. If slides contain automatic build timings, those will be used.

For this task, choose Self-Playing Movie.

4   Set the Slide Duration to 10 seconds and the Repeat option to Loop.

5   Set the movie to fill the screen by selecting "Enter full screen mode when opened."

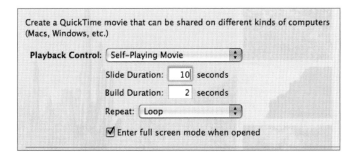

You now must choose playback quality settings for the movie. It is important to keep in mind how you plan to deliver this movie when choosing these options. For example, if you want the user to view the movie over the Internet you'll need a smaller file size. On the other hand, a CD-ROM movie can be larger than a Web movie, but because it has to play back from an optical disc, it should be smaller than a kiosk movie that plays from a hard drive.

6 From the Formats pop-up menu, choose CD-ROM Movie, Medium to set the playback quality.

NOTE ▶ We'll explore custom output in Lesson 11.

7 Since this presentation has no audio, deselect the "Include audio" option.

NOTE ▶ The Include audio option is on by default and can bloat your file size—silence takes up space in your file. If file size is a concern (as it may be for Web and CD-ROM delivery), be sure to disable audio if your presentation doesn't have any.

8 Click the Next button.

9 Give the movie a name and choose the location where you want the exported file to be saved.

10 Click Export.

NOTE ▶ Depending on the number of slides and the speed of your machine, this process can take a few minutes.

11 Navigate to the file in the Finder and double-click the file to view it.

The movie opens in the QuickTime Player application. It should fill your screen and continue to loop (if you used the settings in this task). Because the movie is at CD-ROM quality, the image quality (especially during animated transitions) will be reduced.

12 Press the Esc key to exit the full-screen movie.

13 Quit QuickTime Player and return to Keynote.

Exporting to PowerPoint

In Lesson 4, you imported a Microsoft PowerPoint presentation and enhanced it. This is usually the desired workflow when using PowerPoint files. However, you can build a presentation in Keynote and then save it as a PowerPoint file.

This can help you if you are creating a presentation that you need to send to a Windows user for additional editing.

1   With your presentation open, choose File > Export. Click PowerPoint.

2   Click Next. Then give the slideshow a name and choose a location for the file.

3   Click Export.

Note that PowerPoint handles graphics differently than Keynote, so there may be slight variations in the exported slideshow (especially on a Windows computer). PowerPoint also does not support some Keynote features—for example:

▶   Some bulleted text may be lost when you export a Keynote document to PowerPoint. Don't hide the bulleted text on a slide (by deselecting the Body check box in the Slide Inspector).

▶   PowerPoint does not recognize alpha-channel graphics. Features like photo cutout frames and transparent images will not work properly.

▶   Certain builds and transitions are unique to Keynote and will not export.

Exporting to PDF

The PDF file format has become the format of choice for creating documents that are easy to share among people using a variety of computer platforms and software applications, but that retain their original appearance (including fonts and images). PDF files can be viewed on computers running OS X, Windows, and even Unix as well as on some mobile devices such as PDAs and cell phones. Exporting your Keynote presentation as a PDF file is a great way to distribute your slides or speaker notes.

1   With your presentation open, choose File > Export. Click the PDF button.

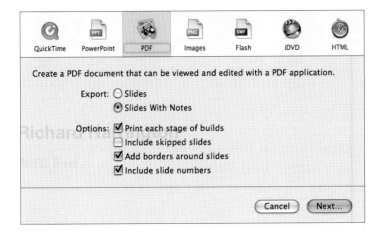

TIP   You can also create PDFs when printing speaker notes. Just click the PDF button in the Print dialog box and choose Save as PDF.

2   Select either Slides (to print slides only) or Slides With Notes. Then select any of the following print options that you want:

► Print each stage of builds: Creates a separate image for each stage of an object build.

► Include skipped slides: Includes skipped slides in the PDF file.

► Add borders around slides: Shows borders around slides.

► Include slide numbers: Shows slide numbers next to each thumbnail.

3   Click Next. Then give the PDF file a name and choose a location for the file.

4 Click Export.

> **TIP** If the PDF will be used as a hard copy printout, use the Print command. Choose File > Print and choose Save as PDF from the PDF pop-up menu.

> **TIP** Keynote does not give you control over the file size of the PDF. If you need to optimize the file for the Internet, you can use Adobe Acrobat (the full version, not the Reader application). You can choose File > Reduce File Size to optimize the PDF for the Web.

Exporting Images

Keynote gives you flexible export options to save your slides as graphics—very useful for preparing images for inclusion in a page layout program (such as Pages or InDesign). This option is also useful if you want to send slides in email or archive them in your iPhoto library.

1 With your presentation open, choose File > Export. Click Images.

2 Select the images you want to export; you can specify all the slides or a page range.

3 Specify any other export options you want.

> ▶ If you want to create a separate image for each stage of an object build, select "Create an image for each stage of builds."

> ▶ If you want to export your slide images directly into iPhoto, choose "Export images into iPhoto." You will be prompted to name the album.

For this presentation, these options aren't needed.

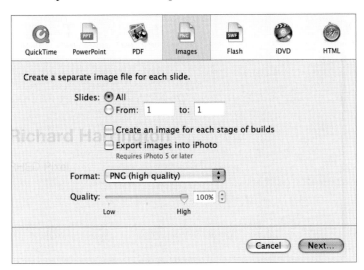

4   Choose a file format from the Format pop-up menu:

▶   JPEG: JPEG files support variable compression rates that can be optimized for Internet delivery.

▶   PNG: PNG files work well for multimedia use and support embedded transparency.

▶   TIFF: TIFF files work well for print projects.

5   Click Next. Then give the file a name and choose a location for the exported file.

6   Click Export.

Exporting to Flash

By exporting to Flash, you can create an interactive presentation with a relatively small file size (note that using lots of photos will increase the size of the

Flash file). Additionally, the Flash file format is very compatible with most Web browsers. Most computer manufacturers preinstall Flash on all systems. Recent surveys show that Flash has a 98 percent install rate on computers that are used to access the Internet. With such a high installed base, Flash is a great distribution option.

Keynote allows you to turn your slideshow into a Flash document. This file can then be viewed using the Flash viewer or browser plug-in.

1   With your presentation open, choose File > Export. Click Flash.

2   If you want to include audio in your Flash document, select "Include the slideshow audio file (soundtrack)."

3   Click Next. Then type a name for the file and choose a location for the file.

4   Click Export.

   A file in Flash format (with the file extension "swf") will be written to disk.

   NOTE ▸ Slide transitions are not included in the Flash export.

   TIP If you need to edit the Flash file, you'll need Flash (which is now sold by Adobe). Choose File > Import > Import to Stage to bring the presentation SWF file into Flash.

Sending to iDVD

As a backup, you might want to publish your presentation to a DVD. You can also create DVDs to distribute your presentation to people who could not attend. Support for iDVD is new to Keynote and requires both iWork '06 and iLife '06. Here, you'll create a DVD of the photo presentation, including a menu.

1   With your presentation open, choose File > Export. Click iDVD.

2   Specify the size of the video you want to create:

▶   Standard: Exports slides for viewing on a standard video display. Use this option if your original presentation has a 4:3 aspect ratio, using a resolution such as 800 × 600 or 1024 × 768.

▶   Widescreen: Exports the slides for viewing on a widescreen video display. Use this option if your original presentation has a 16:9 aspect ratio, as is used by HD displays.

For our presentation, choose Widescreen (16:9).

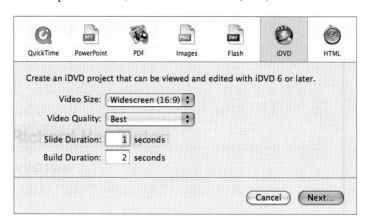

3   From the Video Quality pop-up menu, choose a quality setting.

A setting of Best or High works well for most presentations.

4   Specify the number of seconds you want for slide and build durations.

For this presentation, a slide duration of 1 second will work well. iDVD will add a chapter marker; you will need to click the Play button on the DVD remote to advance each slide.

5   Click Next. Then give the file a name and target your Movies folder.

6   Click Export.

A QuickTime movie file is written to disk. Depending on the number of slides, it can take a few minutes to create the DVD video file.

Before the export finishes, iDVD will launch automatically. Whichever theme you were using the last time you had iDVD open will be active, and you might hear the theme's soundtrack playing. You can click the

Start or stop motion button in the DVD main menu to stop the animation and sound.

7   When the export finishes, click the Play button to test the DVD project:

▶   You can click Play Movie to watch the entire movie.

▶   You can click Scene Selection to see an index of the presentation.

Now let's choose a theme for the main menu of the DVD that matches the look of the slideshow.

8   Click the Themes button to access all available themes.

9   Click the Reflection White theme to apply it to the main DVD menu. Then click OK to apply the theme family to all menus.

Now you need to populate the DVD menu to complete its design.

10 Click the Menu button to access all of the drop zones for the project.

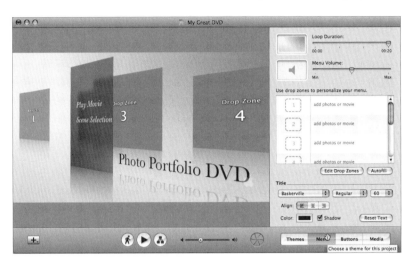

Drop zones are places in the menu where you can add (or drop) your own content. These allow you great flexibility for customizing a menu.

11 Open the **Portfolio Samples** folder in the Lesson 6 folder on your hard drive.

12 Drag the photo **Portfolio 1.jpg** into drop zone 1.

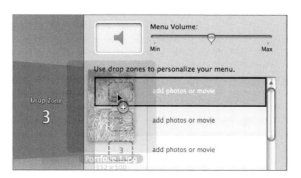

13 Drag the photo **Portfolio 2.jpg** into drop zone 2; repeat for the remaining drop zones until all are filled.

14 Click the font menu in the Title area and change the font to Helvetica Neue Bold.

This makes the font in the DVD menu match the Keynote presentation.

15 Working in the main DVD menu, select the Scene Selection button and press Delete.

This removes the scene selection submenu. If the DVD were longer, this menu would be useful for jumping right to a scene (each scene corresponds to one of our Keynote slides). However, we want the viewer to watch the entire portfolio so we can get rid of this choice.

16 Double-click the Play Movie button in the menu and rename it *View Portfolio*.

17 Click Buttons to access controls for the appearance of the button; then change the Label font to Helvetica Neue Condensed Bold. Then double-click the menu title and rename it *Photo Portfolio DVD*.

18 Click the Preview button to preview the DVD.

Watch the project all the way through to ensure smooth playback. Be sure to click the Play button on the remote control to advance between each slide. When finished with the preview, click the Exit button on the remote to stop previewing the DVD.

19 If you want, you can now click the Burn button to create the DVD.

The Burn button will open to reveal the yellow and black radioactive icon, and you will be prompted to insert a blank DVD. If you'd like to try burning a DVD, insert a blank disc. This step is optional.

20 When you are done with the DVD project, quit iDVD.

Exporting to HTML

Placing a presentation on the Internet has several benefits. It allows you to share the presentation with others during the construction stage, which is useful if you're developing a group presentation or creating one for a client. After a presentation, the Internet is a great place for attendees to find your notes, and posting your presentation can drive potential customers to your Web site.

Creating a Web page with Keynote is very easy. We are still working with **06Photo Portfolio.key** in the Lesson 06 folder.

1 With your presentation open, choose File > Export. Click HTML.

2 For Slides, select All.

You're going to export all the slides to the Web site.

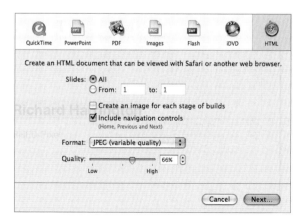

3 To include navigation controls (which is a good idea), select "Include navigation controls."

This adds Home, Previous, and Next navigation buttons.

4 For maximum compatibility with all Web browsers, choose to use the JPEG file format.

5 Adjust the compression quality to suit your needs.

A value between 50% and 80% is usually acceptable for most uses.

6 Click Next. Then name the Web page **Photo Portfolio** and choose a location for the exported file.

7 Click Export.

The Web page takes a few moments to generate.

The page can now be viewed by opening the HTML file you created.

NOTE ▶ One drawback of the export module for the Web page is that large slides may be cut off by many Web browsers. You can resize the image files in the folder Photo Portfolio using an image editing application.

TIP ▶ If you want more options for your Web page, export still images to iPhoto and then create a Web gallery using iPhoto's more robust tools. You can open the iPhoto album in iWeb for even more options.

Creating a Podcast Using GarageBand

By harnessing both iWork '06 and iLife '06, you can create a podcast from your Keynote presentation—that is, you can create a small audio file optimized for Internet delivery and synchronize your slides as embedded graphics. This is an innovative way to distribute your work. We are still working with **06Photo Portfolio.key** from the Lesson 06 folder.

1 With your presentation open, choose File > Export. Click Images.

2   Select All to export all images.

3   Select "Export images into iPhoto."

4   From the Format pop-up menu, choose JPEG.

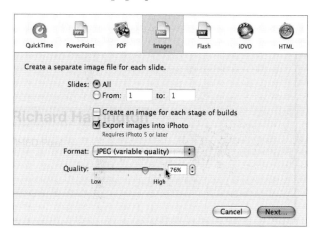

5   Click Next. Then name the album **06 Photo Portfolio** and click OK.

It will take a few minutes to export your slides.

6   Launch GarageBand by clicking its icon in the Dock.

To save a few steps, a GarageBand file has been created and filled with narration. You can explore the full features of GarageBand by picking up *Apple Training Series: iLife '06* and *Apple Training Series: GarageBand 3*.

7 Open the file **06Portfolio_Start.band** from the Lesson 06 folder.

This file contains narration for the podcast and a music bed using a jingle that is built into GarageBand.

8 Arrange your window to look like the following image. Be sure the Media Browser (Command-R) and the Editor (Command-E) are both visible.

9 Click Photos in the Media Browser and then select the **06Photo Portfolio** album.

10 Drag slide.001 into the podcast track. Position the slide so it starts at a time of 00:00:00.000.

You are now going to add your second slide.

11 Click Play and listen to the podcast. When the first photo is mentioned, at approximately 00:00:19.000, press the spacebar to pause the podcast. Drag slide.002 into the podcast track.

This adds the second artwork piece to your Timeline.

12 Continue to add the remaining slides and synchronize them with the narration. When the voice talks about each slide, be sure to switch graphics in the podcast track.

The final artwork track needs an Out point set. This Out point determines when the podcast ends.

13 Position the playhead at approximately 00:03:50.000.

14 Click the podcast track; then choose Edit > Split.

You now need to select the unneeded artwork in the Timeline and remove it.

15 Click an empty track to deselect both pieces of artwork; then select the artwork to the right of the playhead. Press the Delete key to remove it from your Timeline.

16 In the Editor, locate the Artwork column in the marker list and double-click the first thumbnail in the column to open the image in the Artwork Editor. Drag the slider to the left to scale the side to fit. Click Set.

17 Repeat for the remaining artwork.

18 Drag slide .001 from the Media Browser into the Episode Artwork well and double-click the image to open it in the Artwork Editor. Adjust its size to fit as you did with the other images.

It's now time to publish the podcast.

19 Choose Share > Send Song to iTunes.

GarageBand processes the song and sends it to iTunes. In iTunes, click Library in the Source list to display all the items you have imported into iTunes. Find your exported podcast in the library; then select it and choose File > Show Song File (Command-R) to reveal the actual podcast file in the Finder. Once you know where the file is, you can e-mail the file to another person.

TIP ▶ Be sure to explore the Send to iWeb command as well. You can modify the iWeb page and post to your .mac account. See the iWeb documentation for more details.

The following figure shows what your viewers will see when looking at the podcast in iTunes.

You can compare your GarageBand project to the file **06Portfolio_End.band**.

Giving Your Presentation with a Laptop

You will likely be giving your Keynote presentation from a laptop. Using a laptop, you can easily rehearse your presentation at home or elsewhere as well as make last-minute changes. Apple currently sells MacBook Pro, PowerBook, and iBook laptops. Depending on your particular model, the steps for connecting an external monitor will vary. Here are the general steps for hooking up a laptop to a projector and giving a presentation.

1   Close your laptop lid so the machine goes to sleep.

2   Determine whether the projector uses a VGA connector or a DVI connector.

VGA connector.   DVI connector.

A DVI connector is a more modern connector and is standard on most Mac laptops. You may need to use an adapter (likely included with your laptop).

NOTE ▶ Different models of Mac laptops have different connector options. Most laptops ship with an Apple DVI-to-VGA display adapter. If your laptop has a mini DVI port, you will need an Apple Mini-DVI–to–DVI adapter. These adapters are included with Apple laptops and should be carried in your laptop bag. If you lose them, you can buy replacements from the Apple Store.

3   If needed, connect the DVI-to-VGA or Mini-DVI–to–DVI adapter to your laptop.

4   Connect the cable from the projector to your laptop (if needed, use the adapter).

5   Open the lid to your laptop and give the computer a minute to detect the display.

If the laptop does not communicate with the projector (in other words, if your computer's desktop does not appear on the projector), you may need to configure your laptop to detect the display manually.

6 To force the laptop to detect the display, click the Apple menu and choose System Preferences. Then click Displays.

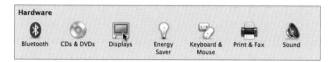

7 Click the Detect Displays button.

8 Select the monitor resolution that matches your slideshow resolution. You can check your slide size in the Document Inspector.

If the exact resolution is not available, choose the closest size.

9 Switch back to Keynote.

10 Choose Keynote > Preferences.

11 Click Slideshow and select the "Present on secondary display" option.

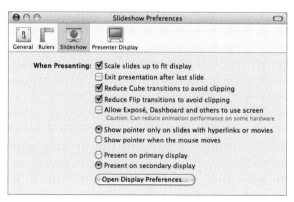

12 Click Presenter Display and select "Use alternate display to view presenter information."

13 Close the Preferences window.

14 Click Play and test your slideshow.

> **TIP** A remote control lets you move away from the computer when presenting. There are several third-party remote controls that work with Keynote. Newer model Macs are shipping with the Apple Remote that can also be used to advance slides in a presentation.

Lesson Review

1. How can you print presenter notes?

2. How can you export your presentation as a movie file?

3. Which four Internet-ready formats can Keynote export?

4. What is a good backup method for exporting a presentation for view on a television or a computer?

5. If your computer can't communicate with a connected display, what can you do?

Answers

1. Choose File > Print; then choose Keynote from the Print options pop-up menu and select Slides With Notes.

2. Choose File > Export, then click QuickTime.

3. Keynote can create QuickTime, PDF, SWF, and HTML files.

4. Keynote can export your project to iDVD so you can create a DVD.

5. Choose System Preferences and then Displays; then click the Detect Displays button.

Publishing with Pages

7

Lesson Files   Lessons > Lesson 07 > 07SourceText.pages

Lessons > Lesson 07 > 07Leagues & Classes.pages

Lessons > Lesson 07 > 07Gym Newsletter_FINAL.pages

Lessons > Lesson 07 > Artwork

Time   This lesson takes approximately 90 minutes to complete.

Goals   Select and work with a template in Pages

Replace placeholder text

Edit image placeholders

Resize an object

Crop an image using a mask

Wrap text around objects

Flow text

Format text with styles

Export to PDF

Lesson 7
Creating a Newsletter

Pages, together with Keynote, make up the iWork suite. The two programs are companions, and they share a nearly identical interface. The visual differences between the two programs exist only because Pages has a very different purpose.

Pages is a flexible word processing application with extensive support for layout and graphics.

At its core, Pages is an easy-to-use word processing application. It can be used to create a variety of documents, and it features a wealth of tools, including functions to check spelling, find and replace text, and format text with styles. However, Pages is more than just a word processor. It provides strong graphics support and a robust selection of professionally designed themes.

You can use Pages to easily create a wide variety of types of documents, including posters, postcards, resumes, reports, and newsletters. In this lesson, you will harness a newsletter template and populate it with content. Then you will export your document as a PDF file that is ready for Internet distribution.

Before You Start

Before you start this lesson, you'll need to load the iWork '06 suite onto your hard drive. You'll also need to copy the lesson files from the DVD in the back of this book to your computer. If you've been working through this book linearly, you did this back in Lesson 1. However, if you've jumped directly into this first lesson on Pages, you'll need to complete this process now.

The instructions for loading the software and files are in "Getting Started," the introduction to this book. Once those two steps are complete, you can move forward with this lesson.

With iWork '06 and the lesson files loaded onto your hard drive, you are ready to start this lesson.

Launching Pages

There are three ways to launch the Pages component of iWork:

▶ Double-click the iWork '06 folder in your Applications folder and then double-click Keynote.

▶ Click the Pages icon in the Dock.

▶ Double-click any Pages document.

For this exercise, you'll launch Pages using the first method.

1   From the Finder, choose File > New Finder Window.

> **NOTE** ▶ If you haven't copied the Lessons folder from this book's DVD-ROM to your hard drive, do so at this time.

2   Double-click the Applications folder icon to open the folder.

3   Locate the iWork '06 folder and double-click to open it.

4   Double-click the Pages application icon to launch the program.

Choosing a Template

When you first launch Pages, you are presented with the Template Chooser. The Template Chooser gives you access to professionally designed templates (and any templates you have saved). Templates contain formatting and layout settings to help you present your information and offer a quick way to get a project started.

The Template Chooser contains templates useful for business, marketing, creative, and educational purposes. You can edit templates to include new content, as well as modify color and font styles. Examining templates also gives you a good idea of what is possible using Pages.

Selecting a template is easy:

1   If the Template Chooser is not already displayed on your screen, choose File > New.

2   Select a template. For this exercise, click the Newsletters category and then select the Modern Newsletter in the Template Chooser window.

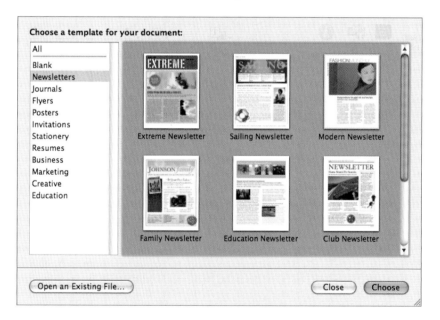

3 Click Choose to open a new document based on the template.

4 Choose File > Save and name the file *Gym Newsletter;* store the file on your local hard drive.

Working with a Template

Most templates contain several page layouts that you can use to quickly format your document. These layouts often contain text, images, tables, charts, and other formatting options you may want. The newsletter we are designing needs a total of four pages. You've already created the layout for the first page; now you'll create the layouts for the other three pages.

1   On the toolbar, click the Pages button, and choose a page design from the pop-up list. For this newsletter, choose the 2 Column layout.

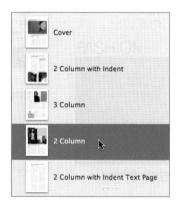

2   Add two more pages to the layout. Choose 2 Column with Indent and Mailer.

NOTE ▶ When a preformatted page is added to your document, a section break is automatically inserted before it. This way, when you edit an individual page it will not affect those that come before or after it.

3 Choose File > Save to save your document.

Replacing Placeholder Text

When you look closely at a template page, you'll notice that the text appears to be gibberish. These words are actually Latin, and this text is usually called Lorem Ipsum text. One of the first things you'll want to do is add your own text to a page by replacing this placeholder text.

NOTE ▶ Using Lorem Ipsum text as a placeholder has been a printing tradition since the 1500s. Lorem Ipsum text can be used to fill a template with content to make it look full. For more on Lorem Ipsum, check out www.lipsum.com.

1 In the thumbnail view, click the Page 1 thumbnail.

If you can't see thumbnails, click the View button in the toolbar and choose Show Page Thumbnails.

2 Double-click the Masthead (it currently says **FASHION**MONTHLY).

3 Type *SMB Member News.*

Using the default font size of the template, the text is too large and wraps to a second (hidden) line.

4 Select the letters SMB; then press Command-B to make the letters bold.

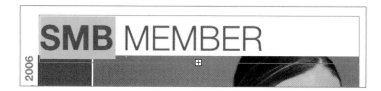

5 Choose Edit > Select All to choose the entire headline.

You need to reduce the size of the letters to fit on one line.

6 Click the Fonts button to open the Font panel.

The text is too large so it needs to be modified so it all fits on a single line.

7 Adjust the point size of the letters to approximately 52 so that all three words fit on one line.

8 Double-click the date along the left of the page to edit it. It rotates into a horizontal position for greater ease in editing. Then enter the current date.

When you're finished, click an empty area of the canvas so the text rotates back into place.

To speed up the rest of the text entry for this document, you can open the source file **07Source Text.pages** in the Lesson 07 folder. This contains all of the text you'll need to use for this project.

9 Copy the Photo Caption text from page 1 of the source document onto your clipboard. Select the text and choose Edit > Copy.

10 Return to the newsletter and select the text in the photo caption area on page 1.

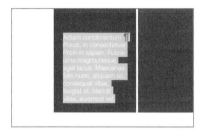

11 Choose Edit > Paste and Match Style.

This adds the text from your clipboard, but maintains the formatting on the template page.

12 Select the story title; then type *Choosing a Personal Trainer*.

13 Click once on the second headline and press Delete to remove the text; then press Delete again to remove the blank line. Repeat for the author byline for the story.

14 Select the story text from the Source Text document and copy it to your clipboard.

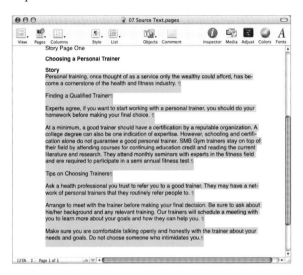

15 Switch back to your newsletter and select all of the text in the story text block on page 1.

Click the first paragraph and drag through all three columns to select the text.

16 Choose Edit > Paste and Match Style to paste the text into your story text block.

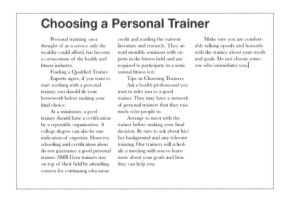

The text can be better formatted to fill up the space on page 1.

17 Select all of the text in the story text block and press Command-= (equals sign) to increase the point size by one point.

> **TIP** ▶ Think of the shortcut as Command-+ (plus sign), which is at the top of the = key.

You now need to format two subheadlines. These help distinguish different sections of the story.

18 Place the insertion point inside the paragraph "Finding a Qualified Trainer" in the first column; then choose Heading 2 from the Style menu in the toolbar.

> Personal training, once
> thought of as a service only
> the wealthy could afford, has
> become a cornerstone of the
> health and fitness industry.
> **Finding a Qualified Trainer**
> Experts agree, if you want
> to start working with a per-
> sonal trainer, you should do
> your homework before making
> your final choice.
>
> a good pe
> Gym train
> their field
> for contin
> and readi
> ture and r
> monthly s
> in the fitn
> quired to
> annual fit
> Tips

You need to add some space around the subheadline to improve its readability.

19 Open the Inspector window and choose the Text Inspector. Click the Text button and set the following options:

▶ Before Paragraph: 12 pt

▶ After Paragraph: 6 pt

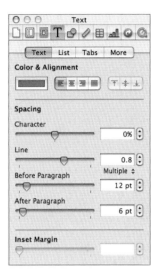

20 Making sure that the insertion point is still within the paragraph "Finding a Qualified Trainer," choose Format > Copy Paragraph Style.

21 Place the insertion point inside the second subheadline ("Tips on Choosing Trainers") in column 2 and choose Format > Paste Paragraph Style.

This applies the formatting from the first subheadline to the second and is a very fast way to format repeating elements.

22 Save your document.

Editing Image Placeholders

You've added the story and headlines to the first page of the newsletter; now it's time to insert the photos. You can add images to your Pages document in several ways (including using the Media Browser, which functions just as it does in Keynote; see Lesson 2.) If you have not added your photos to your iPhoto library, then you'll need to manually navigate to them. So you know how to use both techniques, you'll choose to use the Insert command.

1   Select the large photo on page 1 (the one of the woman on a red background).

2   Choose Insert > Choose to select the file that you want to insert into your document.

3   Navigate to your Lesson 07 folder. Open the Artwork folder and choose the file **01 Cover.tif**; then click Insert.

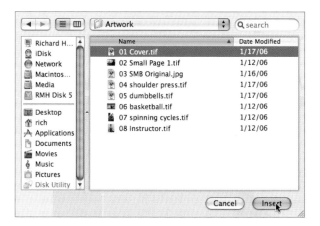

The photo is scaled and added into your page layout. The photo also is cropped to match the shape defined in the template. You can modify this image however.

4   Double-click the image to display the hidden portion of it.

iWork uses masks to hide portions of an image without permanently deleting them. Masks allow you flexibility when altering the shape of an image.

5 Drag the corners of the image to make the image larger. Size and reposition the image so it is better cropped.

For instance, the image shows too much of the windows at the top (you can use the following image as a guide). Cropping helps focus the viewer on the important parts of an image.

6 Double-click the image to return it to just showing the masked image.

7 Save your document.

Cropping Images Using Masks

We still need to add two more images to the first page, but there are no placeholder images left on the page. Nevertheless, we can add more images to the layout.

1 Click an empty area in page 1 so nothing is selected.

2 Choose Insert > Choose; then navigate to the Lesson 07 folder. Open the Artwork folder, choose the file **02 Small Page 1.tif**, and click Insert to add the image to the page.

The image is much larger than we want it to be. We need to size it to fit. Additionally, the image is currently causing words to wrap oddly and making other objects move position.

3   Open the Metrics Inspector and size the image to 1.5 inches wide; then position the image near the top of the large red rectangle along the left edge of the page.

The image is close to the right size, but it needs to be masked. You can mask a photo by using another object as a mask. Here, you will use the red rectangle to create a mask to hide the left and right edges of the photo. To make it easier to see what you are doing, you can zoom in.

4   Click the Page View control in the lower-left corner of the document window and set the magnification to 300%.

This will make accurate masking easier.

5   Select the large red rectangle by clicking it; then duplicate it by choosing Edit > Duplicate.

The red rectangle is duplicated but slightly offset. You need to reposition the rectangle so it is aligned with the original rectangle. This second rectangle will act as the mask for the photo. You need to use a copy of the rectangle since it will be converted into a mask.

6   Drag the new rectangle upward and to the left. Use the alignment guides to determine when the rectangles are lined up. You are trying to place the copied rectangle directly above the original rectangle.

You now need to select the photo in addition to the box. It is possible to select multiple objects.

7   Hold down the Shift key and click the photo so that both the duplicate red rectangle and photo are selected.

8   Choose Format > Mask With Shape.

A mask is added to the photo in the shape of the red rectangle. The left and right edges of the photo are hidden.

9   Double-click the photo to apply the mask.

The photo is masked correctly, but the image is still causing the newsletter title to be pushed to the right.

10   Switch to the Inspector window and click the Wrap Inspector button.

11   Make sure that the small photo you just worked with is still selected, and then, in the Wrap Inspector, deselect the Object causes wrap check box.

Wrapping places an invisible border around the image that causes text to flow around the image. When you turn off wrapping, the headline is no longer wrapped and appears correctly on the page.

You need to add one more image to the main page: the logo for the gym.

12 Choose View > Zoom > Fit Page.

13 Choose Insert > Choose; then Navigate to the Lesson 07 folder. Open the Artwork folder, choose the file **03 SMB Original.jpg**, and click Insert.

The logo is added to the page, but needs to be masked, sized, and positioned.

First, we'll add a circular shape to the document, which we'll use as a mask.

14 Click the Objects button in toolbar and choose Shapes and then the Circle icon.

A circle is added in the middle of the page. You will size this circle to mask the logo.

15 Hold down the Shift key and drag the corner handle to make the circle larger.

Holding the Shift key constrains proportions and keeps the circle shape from becoming distorted. Size and position the circle so it covers the circular logo.

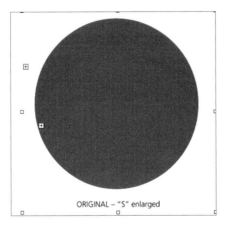

ORIGINAL – "S" enlarged

TIP You can lower the opacity of the circle in the Graphics Inspector to make it easier to position.

16 Hold down the Shift key and click the logo to select it as well.

Even though you can't see the logo, just click right outside the circle to select the logo.

17 Choose Format > Mask With Shape to crop the logo to a circular shape; then double-click to apply the mask.

The body text wraps around the logo and spills onto a new page. You need to scale the logo smaller so it fits in the lower-left corner of the page.

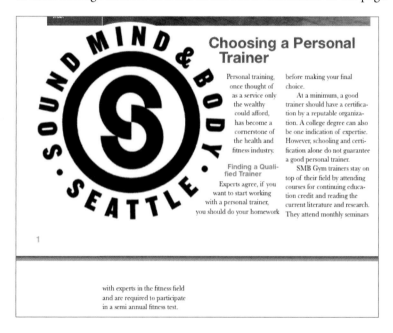

18   Resize the logo so the three columns of text fit on page 1 and the left edge of the logo is aligned with the left edge of the date text block. Position it so it closely resembles the layout shown here.

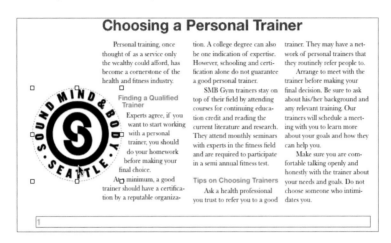

19   Save your document.

Customizing Colors

You can customize the colors in your document—to match the corporate colors of a company, to use colors associated with a season or event, or just to create a better design. Changing colors is easy using the Colors window.

1   Select the small photo on page 1 and choose Arrange > Send to Back.

You're going to change the color of the red rectangle, and moving the masked photo to the back makes the rectangle easier to access.

2   Select the large red rectangle.

3   Click the Colors button in the toolbar to open the Colors window.

4 Click the magnifying glass icon in the Colors window; then click the blue ball in the main photo.

The sampled color is loaded in the Colors window.

5 Click the sampled color strip and drag a small swatch of color into the red rectangle to change its color.

The rectangle now matches the blue of the ball. Next, you're going to change the color of the newsletter title and main headline to match another color in the same photo.

6 Send the blue rectangle to the back of your document by choosing Arrange > Send to Back.

7 Triple-click the newsletter title text to select it.

8 Click the magnifying glass icon in the Colors window; then click the green shirt in the main photo.

The text changes color to match.

9 Triple-click the headline text to select it.

10 Click the magnifying glass icon in the Colors window; then click the green shirt.

The text changes color to match.

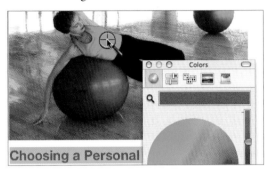

The first page is now complete and has been fully customized for your project.

11 Save your document.

Laying Out More Pages

Now that you've had some practice, you'll find completing the newsletter to be a much easier task. The newsletter has three additional pages. Each has a unique layout, but all require techniques similar to those used for page 1.

1   Select the thumbnail for page 2 to switch to that page.

2   Double-click the edge text that identifies the newsletter and date.

3   Add the title *SMB MemberNews – May 30, 2006* and change the typeface of the first word to bold. The text style keeps the word in ALL CAPS.

4   Select the large picture of the woman and choose Insert > Choose. Then navigate to the Lesson 07 folder. Open the Artwork folder, choose the file **04 shoulder press.tif**, and click Insert.

The new picture replaces the placeholder image. It is sized correctly, but it looks a bit washed out.

5   Click the Adjust button to open the Adjust Image window.

6   Drag the Saturation slider to the right (a value of approximately 70 should be right). The colors in the image now have greater richness and depth.

7 Click the Auto Levels button to adjust the gradations of tone within the image.

The computer attempts to properly balance the relative amounts of light and dark in the image.

8 Close the Adjust Image window.

9 Select the placeholder image (the shoes) and replace it using the same technique as in steps 4 to 7. Use the file **05 dumbbells.tif** from the Artwork folder.

We have two stories to fit on this page. A little bit of formatting will make the two stories easier to read.

10 Select both headlines in the text area by clicking and dragging so they are highlighted.

11 Select the Layout Inspector and change Columns to 2.

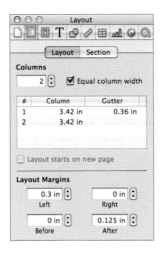

The two headlines are now split into separate columns.

12 Change the first headline to *Total Body Turnaround* and the second one to *Free Blood Pressure Test*.

The first headline is hyphenated, which splits the words so more characters fit on the first line. In this case, we want to reduce the size of the headlines so they fit on one line each and so they match.

13 Highlight the words "Total Body Turnaround" and then press Command- – (minus) to reduce the size of the text.

Press this key combo four times (so that the text fits on one line).

14 Select the Text "Free Blood Pressure Test" and press Command- – (minus) four times.

This reduces the size of the text to match the other headline. Delete the byline text from the second column (the words identifying the author of the story).

15 Click in the green area above the dumbbells image and type the following text:

For more information, visit: www.totalbodyturnaround.blogspot.com

16 In the Text Inspector, click the Align Text to Bottom button.

This aligns the text to the bottom of the green box.

17 Switch to the **07 Source Text.pages** document that you've used before.

18 Copy the page 2 Story #1 & #2 text to the clipboard by selecting it and choosing Edit > Copy.

19 Switch back to the newsletter and paste the story text into the first column of page 2 by selecting all of the existing text and choosing Edit > Paste and Match Style.

The text for both stories is added to the layout and spreads over both columns. The second story about high blood pressure does not begin at the start of the second column.

20 Click in front of the fourth paragraph ("It is estimated that 65 million…").

Total Body Turnaround

Have you tried to make changes in your weight and fitness and feel like you are losing ground? Do you need a change right now? Total Body Turnaround, a 12-week exercise and nutrition program, will change your body and your lifestyle.

This sensible program will help you take control of your eating habits and give you a guided exercise program that works. You will achieve the results you have always wanted and never achieved.

Total Body Turnaround starts on Saturday, January 14 and goes for 12 weeks. If you're interested in joining a group of motivated individuals ready to get in shape and stay that way, join us at a free informational seminar on Saturday, January 7 at 10:00 AM. Sign up at the front desk.

It is estimated that 65 million Americans have high blood pressure. That's up 30% from last decade. This data comes from a report in Hypertension: Journal of the American Heart Association. The United States' population is becoming in-

Free Blood Pressure Test

creasingly more overweight and obese, a key contributing factor to the disease.

Ideal blood pressure is less than 120 over 80. Hypertension, is defined as 140 over 90 or higher. Hypertension can be treated with medicine and lifestyle changes including being more active, eating less fat, eating more fruits and vegetables and reducing salt intake.

Sound Mind & Body has blood pressure cuffs and our personal trainers can check your blood pressure during any of their floor hours.

21 Choose Insert > Column Break to split the columns at the insertion point.

The text is now properly divided between the two columns.

Total Body Turnaround

Have you tried to make changes in your weight and fitness and feel like you are losing ground? Do you need a change right now? Total Body Turnaround, a 12-week exercise and nutrition program, will change your body and your lifestyle.

This sensible program will help you take control of your eating habits and give you a guided exercise program that works. You will achieve the results you have always wanted and never achieved.

Total Body Turnaround starts on Saturday, January 14 and goes for 12 weeks. If you're interested in joining a group of motivated individuals ready to get in shape and stay that way, join us at a free informational seminar on Saturday, January 7 at 10:00 AM. Sign up at the front desk.

Free Blood Pressure Test

It is estimated that 65 million Americans have high blood pressure. That's up 30% from last decade. This data comes from a report in Hypertension: Journal of the American Heart Association. The United States' population is becoming increasingly more overweight and obese, a key contributing factor to the disease.

Ideal blood pressure is less than 120 over 80. Hypertension, is defined as 140 over 90 or higher. Hypertension can be treated with medicine and lifestyle changes including being more active, eating less fat, eating more fruits and vegetables and reducing salt intake.

Sound Mind & Body has blood pressure cuffs and our personal trainers can check your blood pressure during any of their floor hours.

22 Remove the extra space after the "Free Blood Pressure Test" headline by clicking below the headline and pressing the Delete key.

Free Blood Pressure Test

It is estimated that 65 million Americans have high blood

23 Save your document.

Inserting a Page into a Layout

Sometimes, you'll need to move an existing Pages document into another Pages document. This merging can save you time by taking existing content and combining it with new content. For this newsletter, you are going to replace page 3 with a previously laid-out page.

1 Open the file **07Leagues & Classes.pages** from the Lesson 07 folder.

This Pages document contains only one page.

2   Click the page thumbnail and choose Edit > Copy.

3   Switch back to the active newsletter document.

4   Click the page 3 thumbnail and press Delete. An alert dialog will ask whether you are sure you want to delete the page; click Delete.

5   Choose Edit > Paste to add the thumbnail to the newsletter document.

Completing the Layout

You have successfully completed three of the four pages of the newsletter. The fourth page is a mailer page, which is meant to be used for addressing the newsletter for mailing. It's time to finish the layout and then explore PDF output.

1   Select the thumbnail for page 4 to switch to that page.

2   Double-click the edge text that identifies the newsletter and date.

3   Add the title *SMB MemberNews – May 30, 2006* and change the first word to bold.

4   Select the picture of the woman and choose Insert > Choose. Then navigate to the Lesson 07 folder. Open the Artwork folder, choose the file **08 Instructor.tif**, and click Insert.

The new picture replaces the placeholder image.

5   Select the orange box and then change its color to match the pink of the instructor's shirt. Use the same technique as discussed earlier in the section "Customizing Colors."

6   Select the text in the colored block and delete it.

You are now going to extend the colored box so that it appears across the page edge to edge.

7 Select the pink box; then grab the handle in the middle of the left edge of the pink box and drag to the left until it snaps to the guide on the left edge of the page.

The pink box pushes the text out of the way because text wrapping is turned on.

8 Select the Wrap Inspector and deselect the Object causes wrap check box.

The text disappears behind the pink box.

9 Choose Arrange > Send to Back. The text reappears, because it is now on top of the box.

10 Switch to the source text document and copy the page 4 text to your clipboard.

11 Switch back to the newsletter document; then select the text in the pink box and press Delete.

This time we are going to keep the formatting of the copied text.

12 Press Return to add an extra space; then choose Edit > Paste.

The text needs to be indented.

13 Select the text you just pasted into the pink box.

14 Choose View > Show Rulers.

15 Drag the left indent icon (the blue triangle) to the right to the 1-inch mark to move the left edge of the text inward.

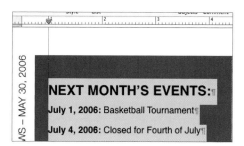

You'll now change the text color to white to improve readability.

16 Open the Text Inspector and click the color well; then in the Colors window choose white.

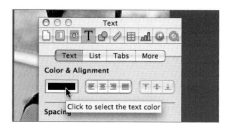

17 Replace the return address in the template with:

Sound Mind & Body Gym

437 North 34th Street

Seattle, WA 98103

SOUND MIND & BODY GYM
437 North 34th Street
Seattle, WA 98103

TIP ▶ Be sure to replace text one line at a time to preserve formatting.

This newsletter is going to be primarily distributed online. Thus, the mailing address area is going to be used only occasionally for sending a few copies.

18 Select the Addressee Name text block and press Delete.

19 Save your document.

Exporting to PDF

Congratulations! The newsletter is complete. It is now time to save it in an Internet-ready format. By sending a newsletter over the Internet, you can save a lot on postage costs. Using the flexible PDF format ensures that your document maintains its appearance and can be printed or viewed by Mac, Windows, and even Linux users.

1 Choose File > Export.

2 Click the PDF button to specify the format.

3 Choose Good from the Image Quality pop-up menu; then click Next.

4 There are three qualities to choose from: Good, Better, and Best. You need to balance file size constraints with image quality when choosing which to use.

5 Name the document *SMB_GYM_06_WEB.pdf* and specify a destination for the file, such as a folder on your hard drive.

It is best to avoid spaces and long file names for files that are meant to be downloaded. The name we entered here identifies the company and the year and indicates that the file is optimized for the Web.

6 Click Export to write the file.

You can now send your newsletter to others as a PDF file.

7 Save your Pages document.

Lesson Review

1. What are two ways to replace a placeholder image?
2. How can you adjust an image's properties after the image has been added to Pages?
3. What's the first step in editing a masked image?
4. How do you stop text from wrapping around an object?
5. How do you scale an object proportionally?

Answers

1. You can drag and drop a new image on the placeholder image, or you can select the placeholder image and choose Insert > Choose and then choose your new image.
2. Click the Adjust button to open the Adjust Image window.
3. Double-click the image to edit its mask.
4. Select the object; then, in the Wrap Inspector, deselect the Object causes wrap check box.
5. Hold down the Shift key while dragging a scale handle.

8

Lesson Files

Lessons > Lesson 08 > 08Nadas Poster_Text.pages

Lessons > Lesson 08 > 08Nadas Poster_Final.pages

Lessons > Lesson 08 > 08Nadas Postcard_Text.pages

Lessons > Lesson 08 > 08Nadas Postcard_Final.pages

Lessons > Lesson 08 > 08Nadas Onesheet Promo_
Final.pages

Lessons > Lesson 08 > 08Images

Lessons > Lesson 08 > 08onesheet text.txt

Time

This lesson takes approximately 2 hours to complete.

Goals

Group objects

Modify fill colors

Crop an image using a shape

Save a template

Export to high-quality PDF

Creating a Marketing Package

One of the major benefits of Pages is its flexibility. Pages supports a wide range of graphic formats and makes moving elements from one document to another easy. You can drag and drop elements or copy and paste them between open documents.

In addition, you can save a layout as a template. You can create a layout from scratch or significantly modify a built-in template. You can then save this custom template so you can use it to create new projects as well as to update the original project.

In this lesson, you will create three items that have a consistent design.

This lesson focuses on the Pages features for creating custom looks and reusing graphic elements. You will learn how to build your own library of assets for your company, band, project, or other purpose so you can quickly create professional-looking marketing tools.

Assembling Project Assets

In this lesson, you'll be creating marketing pieces for a band called The Nadas. You are going to create three items that a band often needs to help market themselves:

▶ A poster, for hanging in live venues and music stores.

▶ A postcard, for promoting upcoming concerts.

▶ An informational one-sheet, for sending to venues for booking and radio stations for promotion.

You can use the same tasks to create marketing tools to promote any event, group, or cause that you work with.

To get started, you're going to add some images of the band to your iPhoto library. This will allow you to easily use the images in your work in Pages.

1   Open the Lesson 08 folder; then open the 08Images folder inside.

The folder contains 12 images that we'll use for this project.

2   With the folder window active, press Command-A to select all of the images in the folder; then drag them onto the iPhoto icon in the Dock.

3 Switch to iPhoto and click the Last Roll button to see the last imported photos.

4 Press Command-A to select all of the images in the roll; then choose File > New Album From Selection (Command-Shift-N) and name the new album *08 Nadas.*

Albums are a tool for saving a group of photos for easy viewing.

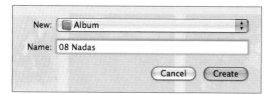

5 Quit iPhoto.

6 Launch Pages.

Creating a Poster

A poster is a common promotional tool. A poster provides a cost-effective way to promote an event, and it offers a large canvas for communicating ideas. Posters are best used to promote just a single event as they are often only quickly glanced at in passing.

You are going to use Pages to create a poster for The Nadas, to promote a concert. You'll also learn how to save the poster as a template so it can easily be updated for future shows.

Selecting a Template

Pages offers three poster styles, and each one comes in two sizes: Regular and Small. The exact dimensions of the poster will vary based on your country, but will match standard paper sizes your printer uses. In the United States, for example, Regular posters are 11 × 17 inches, and Small posters are 8.5 × 11 inches (an acceptable size for a flyer). You'll create a regular-sized poster.

1 Launch Pages.

The Template Chooser opens.

2 Click the Posters category, choose Band Poster, and click Choose.

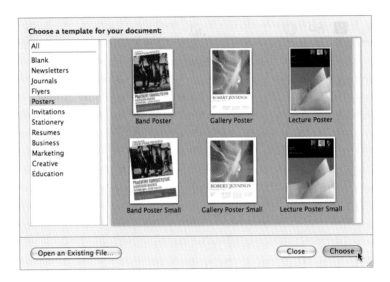

A new, untitled document opens.

3 Choose File > Save; then name the file *Nadas Poster* and store it on your local hard drive.

The poster is ready to be modified to match the style and functional needs of the band.

Replacing Placeholder Text

You need to replace the placeholder text on the poster so that it contains the information needed by the band. This is an easy process that involves just a little typing. We'll work top to bottom, modifying and deleting unneeded placeholder text. Our goal is to change the poster from the template on the left to the finished result on the right.

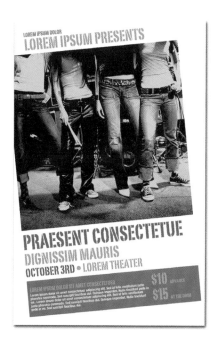

1   Replace the first line of text (Lorem ipsum dolor) with the words *Authenti© Records &*.

> **TIP** To enter the © (copyright) symbol into your text, type Option-G.

2   Replace the second line of text (LOREM IPSUM PRESENTS) with the words *Java Moe's Presents*.

3 Click outside the text block to restore it to the angle defined in the template.

4 Replace the next text block below the photo with the following text:

The Nadas

W/ Special Guest Towncrier

June 8 • Court Avenue

5 Click outside the text block to restore it to the angle defined in the template.

6 Click in the text block at the bottom and delete all of the text except the price information.

You are now going to modify the price information.

7 Select the text block for the price information and duplicate it by pressing Command-D; then drag the duplicate block to the left as shown in the following figure.

8 Modify the text blocks so one says *AT THE DOOR* and the other says *$10*.

Be sure to retype the text to replace the placeholder text.

9 Select the AT THE DOOR text block and duplicate it by pressing

w text block to say *"Listen Through the Static" available on* e a line break before the word "available" by pressing Return.

text blocks and then open the Wrap Inspector. Deselect the wrap check box.

Wrapping causes objects to flow around each other. Since you are going to manually position the three text blocks close to each other, you don't want wrapping to interfere with your layout.

12 Reposition the text elements to match the following figure.

You can adjust the edges of the text block by dragging to avoid hyphenation.

TIP You can disable hyphenation in the Text Inspector by clicking the More button and checking the "Remove hyphenation for paragraph" box.

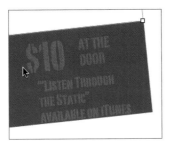

13 Choose File > Save to save your work so far.

Changing Colors and Sizes

The template is well designed, but changing colors and font sizes will further customize its look. Modifying a template is easy, and most of the work can be done using the Inspector, Font, and Colors windows. You are going to use black, red, and white as the principal colors in your design. These colors match the band's latest album cover.

1 For your view, choose Fit Page so you can see the entire document.

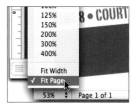

2 In the toolbar, click the Objects button and choose Shapes > Rectangle.

A blue rectangle is added to the center of the page.

3 Switch to the Graphic Inspector and click the Fill color well.

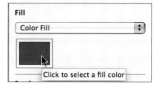

4 Change the fill color to black.

You now need to size the box to fill the page.

5 Switch to the Metrics Inspector and enter the following information:

▶ Width: 11 in

▶ Height: 17 in

▶   Position X: 0 in

▶   Position Y: 0 in

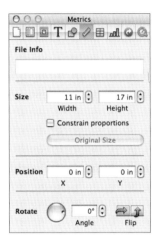

The black box now fills the page and is centered. It is also covering all of the elements of the template.

6   Choose Arrange > Send to Back.

The black box now provides the background for your document. It can now be locked so it doesn't accidentally move or get modified.

7   Choose Arrange > Lock.

8   In the Colors window, click the second button to access the color sliders. From the color model pop-up menu, choose RGB Sliders. Enter color information to specify a red that matches the band's artwork—Red: *255*; Green: *22*; Blue: *50*.

These numbers were provided by the band's record label. Clients and groups often use specific colors.

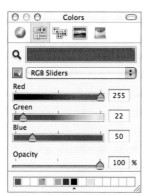

You can store the red color for easy reuse by making it a swatch.

9   Drag the red color from the large bar into the container at the bottom of the Colors window.

10   Highlight the first line of text on the poster; then click a white swatch in the Colors window.

The text turns white.

11   Highlight the second line of text on the poster; then click the new red swatch in the Colors window.

The text turns red.

12 Continue modifying the colors on the page so they match the poster shown here. Use red and white for the text, and use white for the small box.

The layout is very close to finished; all that is left is to adjust the font sizes for readability and style and to add custom artwork.

13 Click the Fonts button to open the Font panel. Adjust the point size of the text on the page. Use the following sizes:

▶ The Nadas: 144 points for the T and N; 120 points for the rest of the letters.

▶ W/ Special Guest Towncrier: 48 points

The third line of text is clipped, we'll fix this in a minute.

▶ $10: 96 points

▶ AT THE DOOR: 36 points

All of the text has been modified, but now you need to clean up the layout. Some text boxes need to be resized to fit their text.

14 Click the text block with the band name; then drag the plus symbol to make the text block larger.

15 Resize the white box to match the following figure.

You can resize your document window to make it larger (and see the space beyond the printed page) or just keep dragging beyond the page's edge.

16 Resize and rearrange the text blocks for the price information to match the following figure. The AT THE DOOR block needs to be larger, and all three blocks need to be positioned.

17 Choose File > Save to save your work.

You can compare your work to the file **08Nadas Poster_Text.pages** in the Lesson 08 folder.

Adding Artwork

The poster design is nearly complete. All that remains is to add custom photos. You will use some of the photos you previously added to your iPhoto library. You can work with your current document or use the file **08Nadas Poster_Text.pages** if you did not complete all of the following steps.

1 In the toolbar, click the Media button to open the Media Browser; then choose iPhoto from the pop-up menu. The contents of your iPhoto library will be displayed in the browser.

NOTE ▶ If you can't see all of the buttons in your toolbar, your document window may be sized too small. You can either resize the window or click the >> symbol in the upper-right corner to access the hidden buttons.

2   Choose the album 08 Nadas to view your imported photos for the band.

3   Drag the photo **nadaspromo** from the Media Browser and drop it on the large image placeholder.

The photo is added to your poster. It needs to be resized to better fill the space. Remember that you can resize the document window to see objects that extend beyond the printed page.

4   Drag the corners of the band photo to resize it. Scale and position the
     photo so it best fills the space between the two lines of text.

5   Drag the file **06 Listen_Through_The_Static_Large.jpg** from the Media
     Browser to the canvas.

6   Open the Wrap Inspector and deselect the Object causes wrap check box.

     You now need to size and rotate the CD cover to match the white box in
     the lower-right corner.

7   Click the white box so it is active; then open the Metrics Inspector. Note
     the angle of the white box (the angle should be 5.5°).

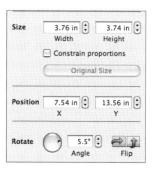

8   Click the CD cover and enter a rotation angle of 5.5° in the Metrics Inspector.

9   Size and position the CD cover to match the following figure.

In this layout, the band photo was moved up so its bottom is flush with the top of the CD image. It is very common to need to tweak a layout to improve its appearance.

The layout is nearly complete. You just need to add some performance photos.

10   Drag the photos **Guitar**, **Perform 2**, and **Perform 1** into the document one at a time.

These photos are all the same size; you need to better size them to fit the layout.

11   Select all three performance photos and, in the Wrap Inspector, deselect the Object causes wrap check box.

12   In the Metrics Inspector, enter a width of 3 inches.

13   Arrange the photos left to right to match the following figure (the photos will overlap some).

TIP ▶ Select all three photos and choose Arrange > Align Objects > Bottom to precisely align the images.

The third photo is being cut off by the middle image. It needs to be arranged to correct this problem.

14 Select the third performance photo and choose Arrange > Bring to Front.

15 Select the three performance photos and choose Arrange > Group.

Grouped objects are treated as a single object. You can combine multiple objects into a group.

TIP ▶ If you change your mind about a group, you can choose Arrange > Ungroup.

16 With the grouped objects selected, select the Metrics Inspector and enter a value of 5.5° (to match the other rotated objects). Press Return to confirm the change.

17 Position the photo strip near the bottom of the poster.

18 Nudge the band name text block up a small amount so that the date and venue information is not cut off at the bottom. Click the text block and press the Up Arrow key.

19 Save your work.

Saving Your Poster for Multiple Purposes

Your poster is finished. Now you'll create a PDF version that you can easily print or send to others. You'll also save your file as a template so you can easily reuse it to create other posters. Documents that need to be frequently updated with variable information (such as venues and performance dates) should be saved as templates.

1 Choose File > Export and click the PDF button.

2 Choose Best from the Image Quality pop-up menu and click Next.

> **TIP** ▶ The PDF format is a flexible format that is well-suited for printing. You can easily print the file from another computer without having to bring your Pages document and fonts with you.

3 Name the document *Nadas_Poster.pdf*; then specify a destination for the file and click Export.

Now save the file as a template for easy access in the future. A template will be stored in your user library and can serve as a starting point for the next poster.

4 Choose File > Save as Template. Give the template a name and click Save.

> **NOTE** ▶ Be sure to use the default location that Pages chooses.

5 Choose File > New to create a new document and access the Template Chooser.

The new template appears in the My Templates section.

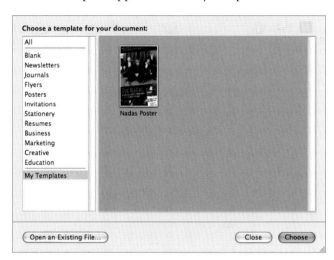

6   Press the Esc key to cancel the new document.

The poster is complete, and you are ready for the next marketing piece in this lesson.

7   Close the document Nadas Poster.

Creating a Postcard

A postcard is an affordable marketing option. Postcards can be mailed affordably, as well as left on counters or packed in with purchases. The postcard is a very popular tool for promoting a variety of events and organizations.

Pages offers a number of postcard templates to choose from. In this part of the lesson, you'll start with one of those templates, but then you are going to substantially modify it to create a custom card.

Selecting a Template

You will first select a template that is similar to the postcard you want to create, so you have a foundation for your customization.

1   Choose File > New to open the Template Chooser. Click the Invitations category, choose Announcement Postcard, and click Choose.

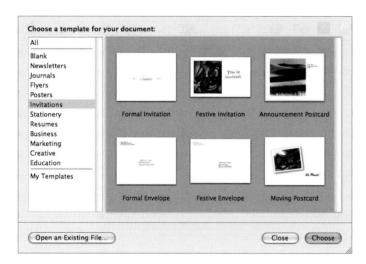

A new, untitled document opens.

The postcard is presented in a 4-up view, which means there are four copies of the postcard on the page, an arrangement that allows you to print multiple postcards efficiently. You will build one copy of your postcard in one of the quadrants, and then copy it and paste it into the other quadrants.

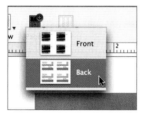

2   Choose File > Save; name the file *Nadas Postcard* and store it on your local hard drive.

The postcard is ready to be modified to match the style and functional needs of the band.

Designing the Card Front to Match the Poster

You want the front of the postcard to be similar in style to the band poster you just designed. It is a good idea for your marketing materials to have a similar look, to help build audience recognition. The front of your postcard will use the same images and colors as the poster.

1   From the Media Browser, drag the Guitar photo to replace the large place-holder photo at the upper-left postcard.

2   Click the text block and press the Delete key to remove the text block from the postcard.

3   In the toolbar, click the Objects button and choose Shape > Rectangle.

    You will use this rectangle as a design element on the page.

4   In the Metrics Inspector, size the square to be 4.25 inches wide and 4.25 inches high.

    This fills the full height of the postcard, and sets the rectangle to be a perfect square.

5   In the Metrics Inspector, set the X and Y positions to 0; then send the object to the back by choosing Arrange > Send to Back.

6   Scale the Guitar photo so it is large enough to fill the card top to bottom.

    You can use the Metrics Inspector to set the height to 4.25 inches and the Y position to 0.

7   Send the photo to the back by choosing Arrange > Send to Back.

8   Hold down the Shift key and click the square to select it.

    Both the square and the photo should be selected.

9   Choose Format > Mask With Shape. Scale or reposition the photo to taste. Double-click the photo to apply the mask.

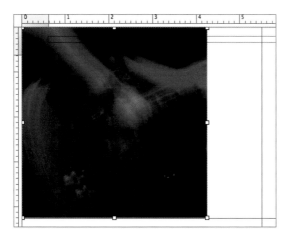

10 In the Wrap Inspector, deselect the Object causes wrap check box.

11 In the toolbar, click the Objects button and choose Shape > Rectangle.

12 Click the Colors button to open the Colors window (if it's not visible). Drag the red swatch you made for the poster and apply it to the square.

13 Drag and position the red box to fill the right side of the postcard. Scale it so it is 1.75 inches wide by 4.25 inches high. Use alignment guides to position the rectangle.

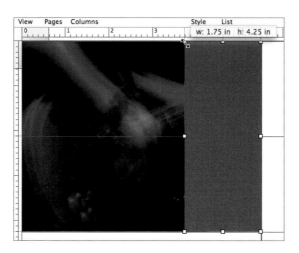

14 From the Media Browser, drag the image **06 Listen_Through_The_Static.jpg** to your document.

The image is very large and needs to be sized to fit into the red rectangle.

15 In the Metrics Inspector, enter a width of 1.75 inches and select the Constrain proportions check box. In the Wrap Inspector, deselect the Object causes wrap check box. Position the CD cover in the upper-right corner of the postcard.

16 Click the red rectangle to select it; then drag the top edge of the rectangle so it is aligned with the bottom of the Listen Through the Static CD cover.

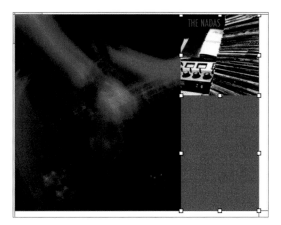

17 In the Wrap Inspector, deselect the Object causes wrap check box.

The front of the postcard is almost complete; it just needs text.

Adding Text to the Postcard

The postcard needs some text information. You are going to create a text logo for the band and add tour information.

1 Click within the red rectangle to make sure no insertion point is showing. Then, in the toolbar, click the Objects button and choose Text; then enter the word *THE*.

2 Select the text; then open the Font and Colors windows and modify the font attributes:

▶ Color: Use the red swatch you saved earlier.

▶ Font: Gill Sans Regular

▶ Size: 30 points

3 In the Wrap Inspector, deselect the Object causes wrap check box.

4 In the Metrics Inspector, rotate the text 180°.

5 Size and position the text box to match the above figure.

6 In the toolbar, click the Objects button and choose Text; then enter the word *NADAS*.

7 Select the text; then open the Font and Colors windows and modify the font attributes:

▶ Color: Use the red swatch you saved earlier.

▶ Font: Gill Sans Regular

▶ Size: 78 points

8 In the Wrap Inspector, deselect the Object causes wrap check box.

9 In the Metrics Inspector, rotate the text 90°.

10 Size and position the text box to match the following figure.

11 Select the NADAS text block and choose Edit > Duplicate.

12 Modify the text block so it says *LISTEN THROUGH THE STATIC TOUR*.

13 Select the text; then open the Font and Colors windows and modify the font attributes:

▶   Color: White

▶   Font: Gill Sans Regular

▶   Size: 17 points

14 Size and position the text box to match the following figure.

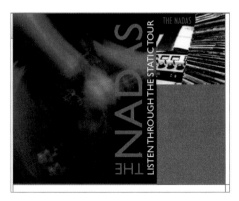

15 Open the file **08Nadas Postcard Text.pages** in the Lesson 08 folder; select and copy the front postcard text.

16 Return to your postcard document. Double-click the red box to edit it; then choose Edit > Paste to add the text.

17 Select the text in the red rectangle and press Command-= (equal sign) two times to increase the point size by 2 points.

The text now more completely fills the red box.

Repeating the Postcard

The card is designed, but needs to be duplicated a few times for easy printing. You will be able to print four postcards on a sheet of paper.

1 Select the elements on the page that are not part of your design and press Delete.

2 Hold down the Shift key and click each element in your new postcard (be sure to select all six elements). You may need to click near the corners of objects as many overlap.

3 Choose Arrange > Group to combine the six elements into a single unit.

4 Hold down Option key and drag the image to the right until its right edge meets the right edge of the page. When a cloned copy begins to move, add the Shift key to constrain the movement.

Pressing Option while dragging an item creates a duplicate of the object and holding the Shift key constrains the drag to a vertical or horizontal straight line.

5 In the Wrap Inspector, deselect the Object causes wrap check box. You will need to click twice.

6   Hold down the Shift key and click to select both postcards. Then hold down the Option key and drag downward until the bottoms of the duplicate cards touch the bottom of the page.

7   Save your work.

Designing the Card Back

You can design the back of the postcard, too, to include additional information. Here, you will add the names and images of the band's albums. To keep the design consistent, you will use elements from the card front. You can use the file **Nadas Postcard_Final.pages** for reference.

1   Click the Next Page button (the down-pointing arrow) at the bottom of the document window to display the second page of the postcard layout.

2   Delete all but the first postcard template on page 2.

   TIP ▶ You can click and drag to lasso multiple elements and then press Delete.

3   Shift-select the three text blocks: for Gallery name, Gallery hours, and Contact information; then press Delete.

4   Shift-click to select the two orange rectangles.

5   Open the Graphic Inspector and click the Fill color well; then, in the Color window, choose the red swatch you created earlier.

The rectangles turn red.

6   Select the two red boxes and the gray box; then open the Wrap Inspector and deselect the Object causes wrap check box.

7   Select the return address and addressee text blocks and press Delete.

8   Open the Media Browser and drag the six album covers into your document.

They are different sizes and too large for the layout.

9   While the images are all still selected, switch to the Metrics Inspector and enter a width of 0.6 inch. Ensure that the Constrain proportions check box is selected. Press Enter to apply the transformation (some of the images will obscure those below).

10 Switch to the Wrap Inspector and deselect the Object causes wrap check box.

11 Position the album covers to match the following figure. Use the Arrange commands to change the stacking order.

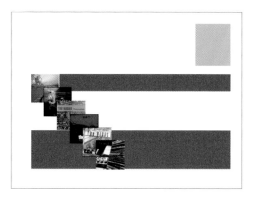

12 Open the file **Nadas Postcard_Text.pages** in the Lesson 08 folder and copy the album titles for the back copy.

13 Double-click to select the text in the top text block; then choose Edit > Paste. Drag the text block down so its top aligns with the top of the upper red rectangle. Drag to the right so its left edge is just to the right of the top album cover.

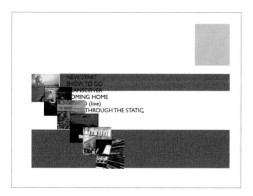

14 Select the Text Inspector and choose the following options to position the text within the text block:

▶ After Paragraph: 11 pt

▶ Inset Margin: 6 pt

15 Adjust the size of the text block to reveal all of the text; then position the text block on the page to align it with the CDs; then choose Arrange > Bring to Front to bring the text forward.

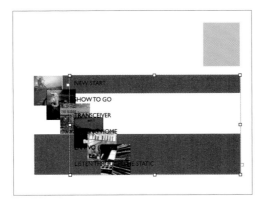

16 Type spaces before the album titles so they are farther from the album images; change the text color of the first title and the last two titles to white.

You now need to borrow some elements from the front of the postcard.

17 Scroll back to page 1 and select one of the postcards. Hold down the Option key and drag a copy to page 2.

The copy of the front of the card is added on page 2 as a grouped object. The front needs to be ungrouped so you can select individual elements.

18 Choose Arrange > Ungroup. Delete all elements except the text blocks containing the words THE and NADAS; then select these two words and choose Arrange > Group.

19 In the Metrics Inspector, rotate the object 270°. Then drag the grouped words into the left corner of the postcard.

The words are too large and overlap the stamp area. You need to size down the text. Fortunately, you can still edit grouped text.

20 Double-click the word THE and change the point size to 24; then double-click and change the word NADAS to 64 points.

21 Ungroup the object. Then reposition the text elements to clean up the alignment to match the following figure.

The postcard design is complete. All that's left is to duplicate the postcard design so a copy occupies each of the four quadrants of the layout.

22 Group the objects for the back of the postcard as you did before: select all elements on page 2 and choose Arrange > Group.

23 Duplicate the postcard and place three copies on the page to fill out the layout.

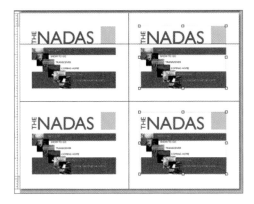

24 Save your work and then close the postcard document.

You can check your work by opening the file **08Nadas Postcard_Final.pages** in the Lesson 08 folder.

Creating a One-Sheet

By now you should feel confident about designing complex layouts using Pages. To test your skills, you can create a one-sheet—a one-page piece that could be sent to venues, newspapers, and radio stations to provide information about the band.

The steps in this task will get you started. From there, you can build upon the skills you've learned in this lesson to complete the project on your own. The goal is to achieve a complex design using several images and text blocks.

1 Create a new document and choose the Blank option. Then choose View > Show Layout.

2   In the toolbar, click the Columns button and choose 2 Columns.

3   In the Document Inspector, change the Margins as follows:

  ▶ Left: 0.5 in

  ▶ Right 0.5 in

  ▶ Top: 0.62 in

  ▶ Bottom 0.62 in

  ▶ Header 0.3 in

  ▶ Footer: 0.3 in

4   In the Layout Inspector, deselect the Equal column width check box and
      modify the width of the two columns:

  ▶ Column 1: 2.4 in

  ▶ Column 2: 4.9 in

  ▶ Gutter between columns 1 and 2: 0.2 in

5   Open the file **onesheet text.txt** in the Lesson 08 folder and copy its con-
      tents to the clipboard and close the document. Return to Pages and click
      in the first column; then paste the text.

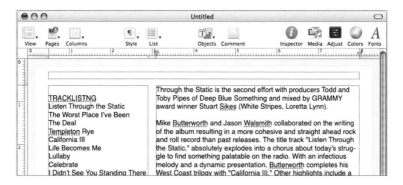

6   Locate the words THE NADAS LISTEN THROUGH THE STATIC
      near the bottom of the first column. Click to place the insertion point
      before the text.

7 Choose Insert > Column Break.

8 Choose File > Save and name the file *Nadas Onesheet Promo*.

9 Open the file **08Nadas Onesheet Promo_Final.pages** in the Lesson 08 folder. Using this file as a guide, complete the layout.

There are still many steps to complete, but you've learned them all already in this lesson.

Lesson Review

1. If you want photos to appear in the Media Browser, what must you do first?

2. How can you join two or more objects together?

3. How can you save a color for later use in the Colors window?

4. How can you rotate text or objects?

5. How can you save a frequently used document layout for quick customization in the future?

Answers

1. Import photos into your iPhoto library; they will then appear in the Media Browser.

2. Choose Arrange > Group.

3. Drag the color into the strip at the bottom of the Colors window and save it as a swatch.

4. Use the Metrics Inspector and enter a specific rotation in degrees.

5. Choose File > Save as Template.

9

Lesson Files   Lessons > Lesson 09 > 09Brochure Text.pages

Lessons > Lesson 09 > 09Tour Brochure Final.pages

Lessons > Lesson 09 > Raw files

Lessons > Lesson 09 > Logos

Lessons > Lesson 09 > TIFF

Time   This lesson takes approximately 2 hours to complete.

Goals   Create a brochure

Add photographs created in advanced image formats

Work with images containing transparency

Lock objects

Work with multiple columns

Creating a Three-Panel Brochure

Three-panel brochures are common marketing tools. They offer a convenient way to convey a lot of information in a well-organized layout. They are also relatively inexpensive to manufacture as they often use common paper sizes.

In this lesson, you are going to use Pages to design a three-panel brochure for a national charity event called the Tour de Cure. You will work with image formats often used by professional designers. You'll need to process the images so they can be used in your Pages layout.

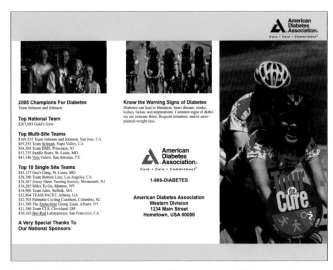

The Tour de Cure is a series of cycling events held in more than 80 cities nationwide to benefit the American Diabetes Association. The Tour is a ride, not a race, with routes designed for all levels of riders. For information, check tour.diabetes.org.

Choosing a Template

When designing a brochure in Pages, you have two choices: Classic Brochure and Three Panel Brochure. The two are very similar well-designed templates. You are going to choose Three Panel Brochure as it most closely resembles other ADA brochures, but you'll depart significantly from the template to match existing marketing materials that the American Diabetes Association already uses.

1 Launch Pages.

   The Theme Chooser should open by default; if it doesn't, choose File > New.

2 In the Theme Chooser, select the Marketing category; then click Three Panel Brochure and click Choose.

A new untitled document based on the template is created.

3   In the toolbar, click the Pages menu and choose Cover without Mailer to add a new page with this format.

This page will be the outside of your brochure.

4   From the Pages menu, choose Inside with 1 Banner Photo.

This page will be the inside of your brochure.

Your brochure now has four pages—the original one and the two you just added. You need to remove the unnecessary pages.

5   Click the View button and choose Show Page Thumbnails.

You can now see a thumbnail of each page in your document.

6   Select the first page thumbnail and press Delete to remove it from the document. Then click Delete to confirm that you want to remove the page from your document.

7   Repeat the deletion for the last page (now page 3).

8   Choose File > Save. Name the file *Tour Brochure* and store it on your local hard drive.

Customizing the Template

The Pages template is a good start. Now you're going to modify it to match the look of other brochures published by the American Diabetes Association. The modification involves two key changes: adding yellow bars and changing the fonts used. Both of these changes are easy to make.

1   With page 1 of the brochure active, click the Objects button on the toolbar and choose Shapes; then choose the square.

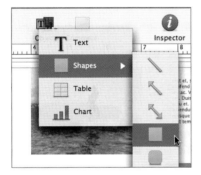

A square is added to the document. It uses the default fill color defined in the template and now needs to be styled, sized, and placed.

2   With the square selected, open the Graphic Inspector. Click the Fill color well to open the Colors window.

3   Click the Color Sliders button, and then choose CMYK Sliders from the pop-up menu.

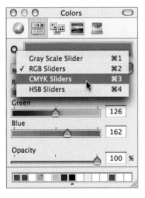

The ADA uses a very specific color of yellow for its materials.

4   Enter the CMYK values shown here to match the ADA-specified yellow.

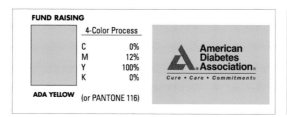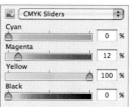

Excerpt from the ADA Brand & Identity Standards Manual.

5   Switch to the Metrics Inspector to turn the yellow square into a horizontal bar and then position it on the page. In the Size fields, enter a width of 11 in and a height of 1 in. In the Position fields, enter 0 for both the X and Y coordinates.

The bar is placed at the top of the page and runs the entire width of the page.

6   In the Wrap Inspector, deselect the Object causes wrap check box.

7   Choose Edit > Copy to copy the top bar to the clipboard. Then switch to page 2 and choose Edit > Paste.

The yellow bar is placed on page 2 in the same place as on the first page. You need another yellow bar across the bottom, but it should be slightly shorter.

8   Choose Edit > Paste to add a second yellow bar; then switch to the Metrics Inspector. In the Size fields, change the height to 0.625 in. In the Position fields, change the Y coordinate to 7.875 in.

NOTE ► The Y value was determined by subtracting the bar height from the paper height. If you're designing using standard 8.5 × 11–inch paper, your brochure will have a height of 8.5 inches: 8.5 − 0.625 = 7.875 inches. Pages rounds the value to two decimal points, but to meet ADA specifications, enter the more precise value.

9 Choose Edit > Copy to copy the bottom bar to the clipboard. Switch back to page 1, and choose Edit > Paste.

The layout template may appear a bit strange as the yellow bars are affecting the columns and text layout. You'll fix this soon.

10 Hold down the Shift key, click the top yellow bar to add it to the selection along with the bottom yellow bar, and choose Arrange > Lock. Lock the yellow bars on page 2 using the same technique; then return to page 1.

Locking objects prevents them from being accidentally moved or modified. Since these bars need precise placement, locking is a good idea.

11 Click in the first column of text on page 1 to select it.

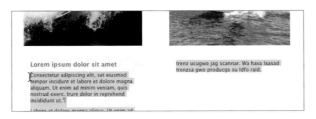

12 Choose View > Show Layout to make the borders of the columns visible.

This will help you size your columns, but first, you need to adjust the overall margins of the document to provide enough room for the columns.

13 Open the Document Inspector and click Document to access document properties. Enter the following values in the Document Margins area:

▶ Left: 0.25 in

▶ Right: 0.25 in

▶ Top: 1 in

▶ Bottom: 0.5 in

14 Switch to the Layout Inspector and click Layout to access column properties. Enter a gutter width of 0.5 in.

The gutter is the empty space between two columns.

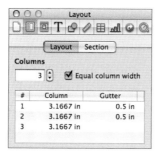

15 Switch to page 2 and click in the first column of text. Repeat the formatting of the columns for page 2 by entering a gutter width of 0.5 in.

16 Switch to Page 1 and click within the blank space between columns to make the page active. Choose Insert > Choose and navigate to the Lesson 09 folder. Open the Logos folder and choose the file **tall_ada_logo_tall_b.eps** and click Insert.

The EPS file (which is a high-quality vector format) is converted to a PDF format file. The logo contains transparency and can be scaled up quite large, as it is a vector-based graphic.

17 Switch to the Metrics Inspector to size and position the logo. Select Constrain proportions and enter the following values:

▶ Width: 1.71 in

▶ Height: 0.65 in

▶ X: 9 in

▶ Y: 0.25 in

The logo now is sized and positioned within the yellow bar.

18 Choose View > Hide Layout since we are done modifying the column layout.

19 Save your work.

Adding Photos

You are ready to add some photos to your layout. Photos may be saved in a variety of formats. JPEG is one common digital image format. Newer digital cameras often used by professional photographers and advanced hobbyists can also save images as *raw* files. Raw images represent the raw data captured by the digital camera and so offer a number of benefits to photographers, including greater editing possibilities using professional image editing applications.

In either case, what you want for your work here in Pages are images saved as TIFF files. TIFF files will import cleanly and do not have much compression compared to JPEG files. While compressed images are good for the Internet, the loss of image quality is less desirable for print usage.

However, here, you have some raw files. You'll need to convert them to TIFF files so you can use them in Pages.

Preparing Raw Files for Import

On first glance, it appears that Pages supports raw files from digital cameras. After all, they can be dragged or inserted into a document. However, Pages converts the images to low-resolution previews that cannot be sized without significant loss in image quality. When scaled, the images become very pixilated (or blocky).

If you have Aperture or Photoshop CS (or later), you can open the raw files and process them. Here, though, we're going to use the tools you have on your Mac to process the raw images, to convert them to the format that Pages needs. These tools aren't as elegant or flexible, but you can use them to get the job done.

> **TIP** If you work with raw files a lot, you should consider integrating Aperture or Adobe Photoshop into your workflow. Both programs give you the ability to organize and process raw files.

1   Switch to the Finder and open the Lesson 09 folder. Open the folder called Raw files.

Inside are two camera raw files. These two pictures were shot with a Nikon camera and have the file extension .nef, to indicate the Nikon Electronic Format (a manufacturer-specific raw file format). Other cameras use different types of raw files, but most can be opened by the Preview application.

> **TIP** Many cameras come with their own software for transferring and converting raw files from the digital camera.

2 Press Command-A to select all of the images in the folder. Then Control-click (or right-click a Mighty Mouse or two-button mouse) and choose Open With > Preview (default).

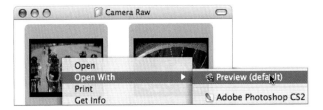

The images open into Preview. Because they are very large files, they may take a while to open.

3 Choose File > Save As. In the Save dialog box, click the column view button to switch views.

You can more easily navigate folders in this view.

4 Switch to the TIFF folder in the Lesson 09 folder and click Save to resave the Riders image as a TIFF file. Remember that TIFF files are better suited for high-quality printing than JPEG files.

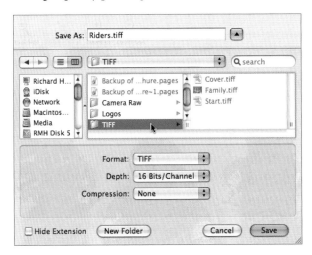

5 Choose Go > Next to advance to the other open image. Repeat step 4 to save the file as a TIFF file.

6 Choose Preview > Quit Preview to close the application and return to your three-panel brochure in Pages.

Importing Photos

Now that the images are prepped, you can add them to your brochure.

1 Switch to page 1 of your brochure and click in the title on the cover of the brochure. The placeholder text is selected. Shift-click the text "since 1977" to add it to the selection.

2 Press Delete.

Beneath the text is a ghosted image that you also need to remove. Selecting it is tricky.

3 Click and hold next to the flowered pattern; drag to the right to select the pattern and then press Delete.

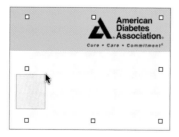

4   There is another flower pattern faintly in the background in the leftmost column on page 1. Remove it using the same technique as in step 3.

5   Click the large surfer image to select it.

6   Choose Insert > Choose. Navigate to Lesson 09 > TIFF > **Cover.tiff** and click Insert.

The new image replaces the placeholder. However, it is very small as Pages automatically sizes it down to fit within the column. If you like, you can choose View > Show Layout to see the edges of your columns.

7   Grab the corner of the picture and scale it to fit between the two yellow bars. Position the image to match the figure shown here.

NOTE ▶ The photo automatically goes beneath the yellow bars because the bars were added after the original photo in the template. Objects added later are in front of those added earlier. You can manually rearrange this stacking order using choices in the Arrange menu.

8   Choose Format > Mask to apply a mask to the figure. Adjust the size of the mask so the photo fits on the rightmost panel of the brochure.

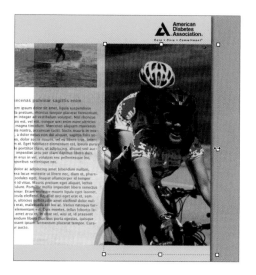

9 Press Return to apply the mask.

10 Select the smaller image of the male surfer in the left panel and replace it with the image called **Family.tiff** from the Lesson 09 folder. Then select the smaller image of the female surfer and replace it with the image called **Riders.tiff** from the Lesson 09 folder.

11 Hold down the Shift key and click the Family photo to select it in addition to the Riders photo. Choose Arrange > Align Objects > Bottom.

The bottom edges of the two photos are now aligned.

12 Press the Down Arrow key several times to nudge the photos down the page. You can add the Shift key to nudge a greater distance. Position the photos to match the layout shown here.

13 In the Wrap Inspector, change Text Fit Extra Space to 15 pt.

The text moves closer to the image.

14 Switch to page 2 and select the large photo of the surfer that spans all three columns.

15 Choose Insert > Choose, navigate to Lesson 09 > TIFF > **Start.tiff**, and click Insert.

The new image is swapped in. The dotted line around the border of the image indicates that the image is masked. It needs its mask adjusted to improve the layout.

16 Double-click the image to edit the mask.

17 In the Metrics Inspector, set the image's angle to 3 degrees and its width to 11 inches. Adjust the mask and the image's position to closely match the following figure.

18 Select the small surfer photo on page 2 and press Delete to remove it from your layout.

19 Choose File > Save to save your work so far.

Adding a Background Image

You can place a photo behind your text as a design element. The image should be simple and lightened so it acts as a texture.

1 Choose Insert > Choose, navigate to Lesson 09 > TIFF > **Wheels.tiff**, and click Insert.

A photo showing a close-up of a bicycle wheel is inserted.

2 In the Metrics Inspector, set the image's width to 11 in, the X position to 0 in, and the Y position to 1 in.

3 In the Wrap Inspector, deselect the Object causes wrap check box.

4 In the toolbar, click the Adjust button to open the Adjust Image panel. Drag the Saturation slider all the way to the left for a value of 0, and set the Exposure slider to 44.

These settings wash out the image.

5 Switch to the Graphic Inspector and set the Opacity to 15%.

This setting makes the image more transparent.

6 Choose Arrange > Send to Back to place the photo behind the rest of the elements in your layout.

7 Choose File > Save.

Adding Text

The brochure is really taking shape. Now you'll add most of the text to the brochure, so you can fit the text into the layout before you size the remaining elements.

Building Page 1

Page 1 is a good place to start. Page 1 contains the brochure's front cover, back cover, and inside fold.

1   Open the file **09Brochure Text.pages** from the Lesson 09 folder.

    This file contains all of the text you need to complete the brochure.

2   Select the text beneath the words "Inside Fold" (from "2005 Champions…" through "…Our National Sponsors"). Choose Edit > Copy.

3   Switch to your brochure and select page 1. Drag in the first column of text to select all of the text in column 1; then choose Edit > Paste.

    The new text is added, but as it is currently formatted; it is too large for the column.

4   Select the first text line ("2005 Champions For Diabetes"). Open the Font panel and change the font to Arial Bold at 12 points.

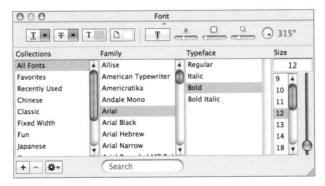

5   In the Text Inspector, click Text; then drag the Spacing: After Paragraph slider to 0 pt.

6   Choose Format > Create New Paragraph Style From Selection. Name the
       style *ADA Header* and click OK.

7   Select the next text line and change its font to Times New Roman Regular
       at 10 points.

8   In the Text Inspector, click Text; then drag the Spacing: After Paragraph
       slider to 0 pt.

9   Choose Format > Create New Paragraph Style From Selection. Name this
       style *ADA Body* and click OK.

10 In the toolbar, click the View button and choose Show Styles Drawer.

You can use the Styles Drawer to quickly access styles and change the font,
size, and style of selected text. Just highlight the text; then double-click a
style in the Styles Drawer.

11 Format the text you just inserted. Use the following sample as a guide. Be
       certain to select all of the text *only* in the first column (the placeholder
       text will return to column 2).

2005 Champions For Diabetes
Team Johnson and Johnson

Top National Team
$267,683 Gold's Gym

Top Multi-Site Teams
$169,535 Team Johnson and Johnson, San Jose, CA
$89,253 Team Schwab, Napa Valley, CA
$84,305 Team BMS, Princeton, NJ
$55,755 Saddle Soars, St. Louis, MO
$41,146 Velo Valero, San Antonio, TX

12 Switch back to the **09Brochure Text.pages** file by selecting it in the Window menu.

13 Select the back cover copy and add it to the clipboard by choosing Edit > Copy.

14 Switch to your three-panel brochure and click in the middle column on page 1. Select both the headline and body text.

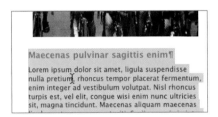

15 Choose Edit > Paste.

16 Select the first line of text ("Know the Warning…") and apply the ADA Header style. Then select the next paragraph of text and apply the ADA Body style.

17 Switch to the Text Inspector, click More, and select the "Remove hyphenation for paragraph" check box to make the text look better.

18 Click in the space above the phone number and press Return five times.

19 Choose Insert > Choose and choose Lesson 09 > Logos > **tall_ada_ logo_tall_4c.eps** to insert the ADA logo.

20 With the logo selected, switch to the Metrics Inspector and set the logo to a width of 2 in.

21 Click to the right of the phone number and press Return to add a line space.

22 Select the logo and the rest of the text (including the phone number and address) by dragging. Apply the ADA Header style; then switch to the Text Inspector, click Text, and under Color & Alignment click the Center text button.

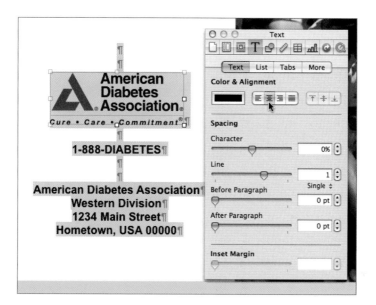

23 Choose Edit > Deselect All to make sure nothing is selected; then click in an empty area outside of any text block.

24 Choose Insert > Choose and navigate to the Tour de Cure logo by choosing Lesson 09 > Logos > **tour_logo_4c.eps**.

25 In the Metrics Inspector, set a width of 2 in for the logo; then switch to the Wrap Inspector and deselect the Object causes wrap check box.

26 Place the image near the bottom of the third column on page 1.

Your completed page 1 layout should closely match the following figure.

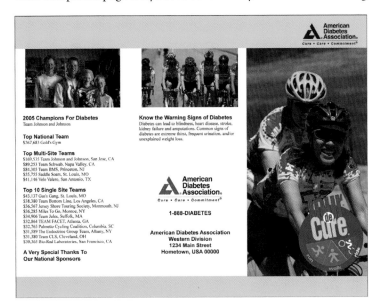

27 Save your work.

Building Page 2

You should be getting quite comfortable working with columns, styles, and images. Completing the interior of the three-panel brochure is similar to completing page 1. It also requires a few new techniques, such as spreading text across multiple columns.

1   Switch to page 2 of your brochure. Delete the large headline and the table from your layout.

The text from the third column automatically flows into the second column to fill in the area previously occupied by the headline and table. This is one benefit of using columns.

2   Switch to the document **Brochure Text.pages** and copy the text beneath the Inside Panels header to the clipboard.

You should be copying three headlines and three paragraphs.

3   Select all of the text in columns 1 and 2 on page 2; then press Delete to remove the placeholder text. Choose Edit > Paste to add the text from the clipboard.

4   Select the first headline ("Race And Family…"). Open the Font panel and set the font to Arial Bold at 16 pt.

5   In the Text Inspector, click More, and select the Remove hyphenation for paragraph check box.

> **Race And Family History Influence Risk Of Diabetes**¶
> You are at an increased risk for type 2 diabetes if you are: African American, Hispanic/Latino, Native American, Asian American or Pacific Islander; Over age 45; Underactive; Over-

6   Select a word in the first headline and choose Format > Copy Character Style.

7   Highlight the next headline and choose Format > Paste Character Style.

8   Repeat step 7 for the third headline.

> **Race And Family History Influence Risk Of Diabetes**
> You are at an increased risk for type 2 diabetes if you are: African American, Hispanic/Latino, Native American, Asian American or Pacific Islander; Over age 45; Underactive; Over-weight or obese; Someone with a family history of diabetes; A woman who has had a baby weighing more than nine pounds at birth.
>
> **Ride Solo Or Form A Team**
> Whether you ride solo or with a team, Tour de Cure is a unique opportunity for businesses, families, or co-workers to come together to fight diabetes, raise awareness, and build a
>
> million people with diabetes and their families. Join 30,000 cyclists around the nation bound by a common cause-fighting diabetes for the health of it!
>
> **Fundraising To Cure Deadly Disease**
> Tour de Cure raises funds to support the essential efforts of the American Diabetes Association to find a cure for this deadly disease. Each mile you ride and every dollar you raise supports diabetes treatment, education and advocacy for adults and children, touching

The text needs to be spread over three columns and it needs to be balanced so that the lengths are more even.

9 Click to place the insertion point to the left of the second headline ("Ride Solo Or…") and choose Insert > Column Break. Then click to the left of the third headline ("Fundraising To Cure…") and choose Insert > Column Break.

The document should now look like the following figure.

There is room to make the banner photo at the top larger to better fill up the layout.

10 Double-click the photo to edit the mask. Click the dotted line that represents the mask, and drag down to reveal more of the photo. Reposition the photo to taste; then press Return to apply the mask.

11 The hyphenation in the three columns is distracting. Use the Text Inspector to remove the hyphenation for each column.

The layout is almost complete. You have just two text boxes to add.

12 Click outside the document pages to deselect all text elements.

13 In the toolbar, click the Objects button, choose Shapes, and choose the rounded rectangle.

A blue rounded rectangle is added in the middle of the page.

14 In the Graphic Inspector, click the Fill color well to open the Colors window; then with the Magnifying glass sample yellow from the top bar.

The fill of the rounded rectangle changes to match the top bar.

15 In the Wrap Inspector, deselect the Object causes wrap check box.

16 In the Metrics Inspector, set the width to 3 in and the height to 1.5 in.

17 Position the box near the bottom of the first column on page 2.

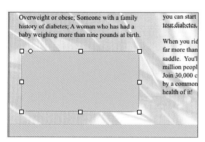

18 Switch to the **09Brochure Text** document and copy the text for the first inside panel callouts to the clipboard.

This text contains a Web address. By default, Pages attempts to automatically format Web addresses as hyperlinks. While this behavior is useful in Keynote, it's less useful in a printed document.

19 Choose Pages > Preferences; then click the Auto-Correction button and deselect the Automatically detect email and web addresses check box. Close the Preferences dialog.

20 Switch back to your brochure layout, double-click inside the rounded rectangle, and choose Edit > Paste.

21 Use the Font panel to change the text to bold. Then switch to the Text Inspector and click the Text button. Click the Center Text button to align the text to the center of the rounded rectangle. Use the Spacing: After Paragraph slider to choose a value of 0 pt.

22 Click outside the active text to deselect it; then select the rounded rectangle and choose Edit > Duplicate to duplicate it.

23 Drag the new duplicate rounded rectangle to the third column on page 2.

Use alignment guides to help you position the box.

24 Switch to your source text document and copy the text for the second inside panel callout to your clipboard.

25 Select the text in the second rounded rectangle and choose Edit > Paste and Match Style. In the Text Inspector, click the Align Text to Middle button.

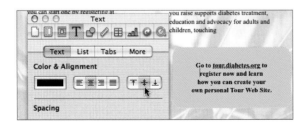

26 Save your work.

You can open the file **09Tour Brochure Final.pages** to compare your project.

Lesson Review

1. How does Pages handle vector EPS files?

2. Can you import a usable raw file directly into Pages?

3. To make sure that an object isn't accidentally modified, what can you do?

4. How can you manually determine where text wraps to another column?

5. How can you apply a Character Style to a selection?

Answers

1. It converts them to a vector PDF with transparency when you import.

2. No. You first need to process the raw files by converting them to TIFF format using Preview. You can also use image editing programs such as Aperture or Adobe Photoshop; these offer advanced options for handling raw files.

3. Choose Arrange > Lock to prevent accidental modifications.

4. Choose Insert > Column Break to wrap text to the next column.

5. You can apply a style by choosing it from the Styles Drawer or by copying the style and then pasting it with the Format menu.

10

Lesson Files

Lessons > Lesson 10 > 10TDC Draft Script.pages

Lessons > Lesson 10 > 10TDC Script Final.pages

Lessons > Lesson 10 > 10TDC Storyboard Final.key

Lessons > Lesson 10 > 10TDC Storyboard Print Final.pages

Lessons > Lesson 10 > Video Script.pages

Lessons > Lesson 10 > Storyboard Art

Lessons > Lesson 10 > tour_logo.eps

Lessons > Lesson 10 > RPLogo.tif

Time

This lesson takes approximately 1 hour to complete.

Goals

Use Pages to create a custom template for a video script

Use Keynote to create a storyboard presentation

Publish a presentation to .mac

Use Pages to create a storyboard handout

Use Pages to create a layout for a proposal

Creating a Script, Storyboard, and Presentation

Computer users working in the film and television and graphic design communities rely heavily on their Macs. If you look in most creative departments and design boutiques, you see Macs being used to create everything from magazines and Web sites to television shows and Hollywood films.

While Macs are well suited for all of those creative tasks, someone had to sell the job. The creative pros (or someone at the company) have to respond to potential jobs, building proposals, and making presentations.

In this lesson, you'll see how iWork can be used by a creative pro to tackle business tasks. In fact, you'll work with materials created for a real-world client to pitch a real-world TV commercial. You'll see that both Pages and Keynote can help you save time and make great-looking presentations to win more jobs.

Lesson 9 introduced the Tour de Cure event—a series of bicycle rides throughout the United States to raise money for the American Diabetes Association. In this lesson, you'll help the ADA create a public service announcement (PSA) for the event for broadcast television. The commercial promotes the event and the riders who participate in it. Before shooting the video, the client needs a script and a storyboard—a walk-through of the video using images and text. Using Pages and Keynote, you will create both of these elements. You will also create a layout for a proposal that you can use with other clients.

Saving a Template for a Video Script

A television commercial needs a script written before it can be shot. While writing a script or screenplay is a difficult task, making it look professional with Pages is not. Pages includes a Screenplay template, but the standard two-column video script was left out. No problem, though—you can easily add a custom template.

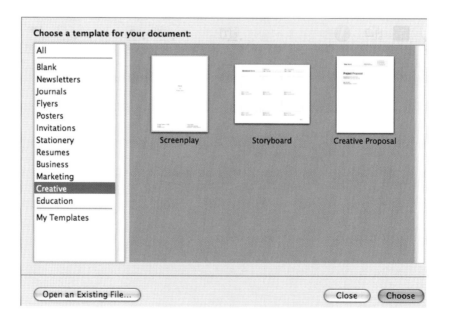

In this task, you will work with a two-column starter script, modifying it and saving its layout as a template for future projects.

1   Open the file **Video Script.pages** from the Lesson 10 folder.

This is a starter script that you can customize. The header of this script contains a five-column table that can hold information about the project. The fifth column contains the organization's logo. Tables are easy to format and modify using the Table Inspector.

The first step is to replace the placeholder logo.

2   Switch to the Finder; then open the Lesson 10 folder and drag the file **RPLogo.tif** into the cell holding the logo.

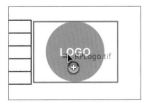

NOTE ▶ Feel free to use your own company's logo if you prefer.

3   Choose File > Save as Template to save the script layout as a template for future projects.

Pages automatically names the template Video Script to match the original file and chooses the My Templates folder in the Application Support folder for iWork. (The complete path to this folder is [username]/Library/Application Support/iWork/Pages/Templates/My Templates.)

4   Click Save to store the template.

5   Close the open document; there is no need to save changes.

6   Choose File > New and click My Templates. Select the newly created Video Script template and click Choose.

A new untitled document based on the script template opens. The body of the document (below the header) consists of a table containing two columns: the left column is for describing the video information; the column on the right is for describing the audio that plays. Both cells in the first row of the table proper (below the header, which contains the labels "VIDEO" and "AUDIO") contain placeholder text.

You are going to format a script properly to present to the client. A description of what will be seen goes in the left column, and the right column contains the dialogue or sound effects.

7   Triple-click the placeholder text DESCRIBE THE SCENE to select it and type *MAN ON BIKE*. To make typing easier, press the Caps Lock key.

All caps is the standard style for video scripts.

8   Press the Tab key to switch to the next column; type the first line of dialogue *63!*.

9   Press Tab to create a new row and switch to it. Enter the description *WOMAN ON BIKE*, press Tab, and enter the second line of dialogue *25!* Press Tab to create a new row.

Agency:		Writer:	
Client:		Producer:	
Project:		Director:	
Title:		Page:	1 of 1
TRT:		Version:	

VIDEO		AUDIO	
MAN ON BIKE		63!	
WOMAN ON BIKE		25!	

10   Open the file **10TDC Draft Script.pages** from the Lesson 10 folder.

This file contains the rest of the text you need to complete the script. You can copy the remaining text (a line at a time) and choose Paste and Match Style.

TIP ▸ If necessary, you can select a cell and choose Format > Copy Table Style, and then select other cells and paste the formatting.

11   In the script header area, enter the following information (or your own) to complete the script:

Agency:	RHED Pixel	Writer:	Mark Weiser
Client:	American Diabetes Assoc.	Producer:	Sara Evans
Project:	Tour de Cure PSA	Director:	Rich Harrington
Title:	How many miles?	Page:	1 of 1
TRT:	:30	Version:	2

12   Save your work by choosing File > Save. Name the file *TDC Script.pages* and save it to your hard drive.

You can compare your document to the file **10TDC Script Final.pages** in the Lesson 10 folder. Leave the script file open as you'll use it in the next exercise.

Creating a Storyboard Presentation

Storyboards are often used to bring a script to life. They use pictures and words—like a comic strip—to tell the story that the video will ultimately film. Keynote can be the perfect vehicle for creating a storyboard presentation. It even includes a template for creating storyboards, which you'll use here.

You'll prepare a storyboard for the script you prepared in the preceding exercise. You'll start by copying the script so you can use it in your work in Keynote.

1   In your **10TDC Draft Script.pages** file, drag to select all of the audio information in column 2. Copy the text to the clipboard.

If you didn't complete all the steps in the previous task, you can open **10TDC Script Final.pages** in the Lesson 10 folder and copy the audio information from there.

VIDEO	AUDIO
MAN ON BIKE	63!
WOMAN ON BIKE	25!
GROUP OF RIDERS	15!
WOMAN WITH BIKE	100!
CHEERING AT REST STOP	EVERY MILE BRINGS US CLOSER.
GROUP OF RIDERS	62!
CLOSE SHOT OF TEENAGER	10!
TIGHT SHOT OF BIKE WHEELS	EVERY MILE IN A CITY NEAR YOU.
MAN DRINKING WATER	

2   Launch Keynote.

3   In the Theme Chooser, select the Storyboard template and click Choose.

A new untitled document based on the theme opens.

4   In the toolbar, click the View button and choose Outline. Then click the Masters button and choose the Photo – Horizontal design.

When you preselect the slide master, Keynote uses it for all new slides. When you paste text in outline view, a new slide is created every time Keynote detects a paragraph break.

5   Click next to the slide 1 icon in the slide organizer. Then choose Edit > Paste and Match Style.

The text is added, and a new slide is created for each line of text. Now you need to add artwork.

6   Save your work. Name the file *TDC Storyboard* and save it on your hard drive.

7   In the slide organizer, click slide 1 to select it.

8   Open the Storyboard Art folder in the Lesson 10 folder and drag the file **01.jpg** into the cutout window on slide 1.

The storyboard artwork is added in the photo cutout.

9   Reposition the image using the alignment guides.

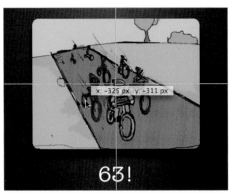

10   Drag the file **02.jpg** into the image cutout on slide 2 and reposition it using the alignment guides.

11   Repeat step 8 for the remaining 16 images. If the text is cut off on a slide, make the text box larger or reduce the size of the text.

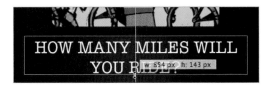

12   In the toolbar, click the View button and choose Navigator. In the slide organizer, click slide 1.

13   Click the New button to add a blank slide.

A new slide is added after slide 1 based on the current master. You are going to build a custom introductory slate that features the client's logo. This will help brand the pitch.

14   In the toolbar, click the Masters button and choose Title – Top.

15 Enter the title *Tour de Cure PSA (:30)*.

Now you'll add a logo next to the title.

16 Click an empty area of the slide and choose Insert > Choose; then navigate to the Lesson 10 folder and select the **tour_logo.eps** file.

The logo is added to the slide but is hard to read. Adding a white box behind it can improve this.

17 In the toolbar, click the Shapes button and add a rectangle. In the Graphic Inspector, choose Color Fill from the Fill pop-up menu. The color white is selected by default.

18 Resize the white square so that it is a rectangular bar that stretches from edge to edge of the slide and is slightly taller than the logo.

TIP ▶ Hold down the Option key while dragging to scale equally in both directions.

19 Send the white rectangle behind the logo by choosing Arrange > Send to Back.

Many clients have logo standards that prevent the addition of glows or shadows to their logos. Placing the logo over a white bar ensures that it is easy to read and still within the client's guidelines.

20 Move slide 2 to the top of the list in the slide organizer so it becomes slide 1.

Now you're going to add a transition between all of your slides.

21 Press Command-A to select all of your slides in the slide organizer.

22 Open the Slide Inspector and click Transition. Choose 3D Effects: Fall from the Effects menu. The same transition will be applied to all of the selected slides. Set the duration to 1.50 s.

23 In the toolbar, click the Play button to view your slides.

You can use the spacebar or mouse button to advance your slides and press the Esc key to exit the presentation.

You can compare your work to the file **10TDC Storyboard Final.key**.

Publishing a Presentation to .mac

When you create a presentation for a client, the client may not have access to Keynote or all of the fonts that you have used. One way around this problem is to publish your presentation to the Internet using a .mac account.

> **TIP** If you don't have a .mac account, you can sign up for a 60-day trial at www.mac.com.

1 In Keynote, make sure that the presentation TDC Storyboard.key is open.

If you did not work through the previous exercise, you can use the file **10TDC Storyboard Final.key**.

2 Choose File > Export and click QuickTime to preserve animations and timings.

3 Choose the following options:

▶ Playback Control: Self-Playing Movie

▶ Slide Duration: 5 seconds (specifies how long each slide stays onscreen)

▶ Build Duration: 2 seconds (specifies how long each bullet holds for)

▶ Repeat: None

▶ Format: CD-ROM Movie, Medium, or Web Movie, Small (depending on the viewer's connection speed)

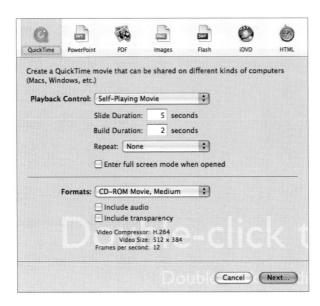

4   Click Next.

5   Give the file a name and specify a temporary destination on your hard drive.

You'll now transfer the movie to your iDisk for Internet viewing.

6   In the Finder, choose Go > iDisk > My iDisk.

7   Open iDisk and copy the slideshow movie into your Movies folder.

Depending on your Internet connection speed and length of presentation, the file may take a few minutes to upload.

8   Launch Safari and connect to www.mac.com. Click the Log In button.

9 Enter your username and password. Then, in the My Pages area of the
   Welcome Page, click More to access all page controls.

10 In the Create a Page area, click the iMovie tab. Then select a template to
   hold your movie by clicking its thumbnail.

   TIP While they are rather plain, the Frameless White and Frameless
   Black templates look very professional.

11 Enter a Web page name, clip name, and description in the empty fields.

12 Click Choose to select the movie file. Then navigate through the iDisk
   folder structure and select your clip.

13 Click Publish to produce the Web page and publish it to your .mac account.

   The next page gives you a Web link to access the movie as well as the
   option to send an iCard to announce the site.

Creating a Storyboard Handout

In addition to presenting your storyboard in Keynote, you will want to leave
physical copies behind for the client. These can be laid out using Pages to create an effective hard copy.

1 Switch to Pages.

2   Choose File > New to open the Template Chooser; then choose the Creative Category and the Storyboard template and click Choose.

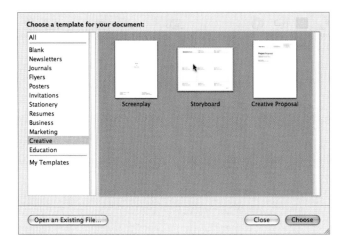

A new untitled document based on the template opens.

3   Enter the information about the television commercial into the header.

Tour de Cure	Client	American Diabetes Association	Title	How Many Miles?
	Spot	English :30	Job #	RP1972

4   In the toolbar, click the Pages button and add a Cover page.

5   Enter the Production information into the body of the Cover page; you can use the Colors window to mix colors or grays into the type.

6   In the toolbar, click the View button and choose Show Page Thumbnails if thumbnails aren't already visible. Then drag the Cover page to the top of the stack so it is page 1.

7   Click page 2 in the thumbnail view. Then, in the toolbar, click the Pages button and add two more pages using the 6 Up Storyboard page.

8   Open the Lesson 10 folder; then open the Storyboard Art folder. Drag the file **01.jpg** into the first empty cutout on page 2 (the first of the 6 Up Storyboard pages).

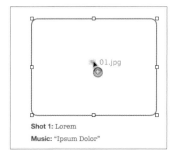

When you release the mouse button, the image is added to the page and scaled to fit.

9   Repeat step 8 for the remaining 17 images. Enter the images from left to right; then switch to the next row of images.

10 Open the file **TDC Script Final.pages** that you created earlier (if you did not work through the earlier part of this lesson, open **10TDC Script final.pages**) and copy the text for shot 1 (63!) to the clipboard.

11 Switch back to the storyboard and select all of the placeholder text below shot 1 and choose Edit > Paste.

12 Use the Text Inspector and Font window to format the text to taste. Consider making the text larger, and center it both top to bottom and horizontally within the cell.

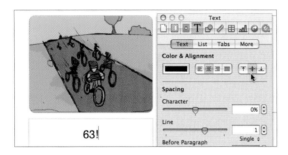

13 Add the remaining lines of the script to the appropriate pictures.

14 Save your work. Name the file *TDC Storyboard Print* and save it in the Lesson 10 folder.

You can compare your file to **10TDC Storyboard Print Final.pages.**

The storyboard can now be printed or exported to PDF for emailing to the client.

15 To print, choose File > Print and select your printer.

You may want to adjust your printer to print the image at high quality so the colors are rich and saturated.

16 To create a PDF file, choose File > Export to open the Export dialog box. Click PDF and choose Good from the Image Quality pop-up menu. Click Next, and in the dialog box name the file *TDC Storyboard Print* (the extension "pdf" will be added automatically) and save it on your hard drive.

Laying Out a Proposal

You'll often need to pull project ideas, company information, and budgets into a proposal. The task of laying out a proposal is well suited to Pages. In fact, Pages gives you several proposal templates (or templates that will work) in the Template Chooser:

- ▶ Business > Project Proposal
- ▶ Creative > Creative Proposal
- ▶ Marketing > Program
- ▶ Marketing > Datasheet
- ▶ Marketing > White Paper

You'll work with the Creative Proposal template here.

> **NOTE** ▶ The art of writing a good proposal is beyond the scope of this book, but you can browse the business section of a bookstore to find ideas and sample proposals.

1   Continue working in Pages (or launch it if you quit the program).

2   If it's not visible, open the Template Chooser by selecting File > New. Choose the Creative category, select the Creative Proposal, and click Choose.

A new untitled document based on the template opens.

> **NOTE** ▶ Pages automatically inserts your personal contact information into the appropriate fields on the page. It obtains this information from the database maintained by the Address Book application included with Mac OS X.

3   Select the personal name placeholder text and press the Delete key.

4   Into the position where the name used to appear, drag a company logo. You can use the file **RPLogo.tif** from the Lesson 10 folder.

5   Repeat the addition of the logo to the header on page 2.

6   Continue adding pages as needed by clicking the Pages button in the toolbar.

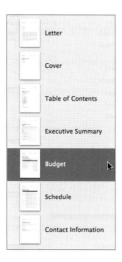

7   Continue practicing with the template, adding photos if you want. Here are some tips for using Pages for your proposals:

▶   The executive summary page can serve as both a summary and an outline for your presentation. You can create a short version as a summary and then use the headers on the page as an outline for your proposal.

▶   The budget template is all set up with tables and calculations. Just change the quantity or unit price to calculate the project budget.

▶   A schedule is important in your proposal. Changes in delivery time are among the key factors that determine project costs and success.

▶   Be sure to add a contact information page at the end of your proposal so people can get in touch.

8   When you're finished, you can save the document for future use or close it without saving.

This exercise will be much more meaningful if you put the template into action and use it for your next project proposal.

TIP If you customize a proposal a lot, consider saving it as a template (File > Save Template). It's also a good idea to keep old proposals for reference and source images.

Lesson Review

1. How can you save a layout as a template for future use?

2. Where can you find your custom templates?

3. How can you apply a table's formatting to all cells of a table?

4. How can you apply a slide transition to every slide in a Keynote presentation?

5. How can you save a smaller PDF file to e-mail?

Answers

1. Choose File > Save as Template.

2. User-created templates are stored in the My Templates folder by default.

3. Select a table's cell and choose Format > Copy Table Style, then select the cells in the table that need formatting and choose Format > Paste Table Format.

4. Select all of your slides in the slide organizer, then choose a transition in the Slide Inspector.

5. Choose File > Export and click PDF. Select Good from the Image Quality pop-up menu and click Next to name and Save the file.

For the Power User (Bonus Lesson)

One of iWork's strengths is its easy integration with iPhoto, iTunes, and the other iLife applications. Creative professionals can take Keynote and Pages even further by using it in conjunction with Adobe Photoshop and Apple's Final Cut Studio suite.

Lesson 11, located on the DVD in PDF form, offers some advanced techniques for using iWork with other applications to create even more sophisticated content. Because Pages and Keynote support embedded alpha channels, it's relatively easy to incorporate advanced content into your page layouts and presentations. If you don't have all of the applications mentioned in this lesson, you can still follow along by using the finished media files provided on the DVD.

Open **Bonus Lessons > Lesson 11** on the DVD. You'll learn how to:

▶ Convert RAW image files from your Aperture library for use in Keynote or Pages

▶ Use LiveType to animate text for a Keynote presentation

▶ Create a motion background with LiveType and integrate it into a presentation

▶ Compress video for your presentations using QuickTime Pro or Compressor

▶ Create a particle-based animation in Motion to accent a Keynote slide

▶ Create a PANTONE color strip in Photoshop and import it to more closely match PANTONE colors in Keynote and Pages

▶ Import a layered Photoshop file into Keynote or Pages

▶ Export an animated Keynote chart as a self-playing movie for use in a Final Cut Pro video project

Appendix

Organizing and Refining Your Photos (iLife Bonus Lesson)

In this book, we've scratched the surface of what you can do with iLife '06. For those who want to delve deeper into the iLife suite of applications, we've included a bonus iLife '06 chapter on the DVD.

Excerpted from *Apple Training Series: iLife '06* by Michael Rubin, the sample chapter focuses on iPhoto and photography and covers how to:

► Make custom albums of photographs

► Organize your photographs within albums and folders

► Improve and adjust the look of your photographs

To get started, open **Bonus Lessons > iLife Lesson 3**. You'll find the lesson as a PDF file and a folder containing the media you'll need to complete the lesson.

If you enjoy the sample chapter, you can order *Apple Training Series: iLife '06*, or get a complete list of Apple Pro Training Series titles by visiting www.peachpit.com/appleprotraining.

Index

Symbols

= (equals sign)
    for navigating slide switcher, 105
    in table calculations, 40–41
/ (forward slash), 106
– (minus sign), 106
+ (plus symbol)
    in formatting text in shapes, 27–28
    for navigating slide switcher, 105
? (question mark), 106
] (right bracket), 105

A

AAC files
    adding to slideshow, 64
    creating in iTunes, 66–67
Adobe Acrobat, controlling PDF file size, 214
Adobe Photoshop. *See* Photoshop
advanced techniques, DVD:1–DVD:32
    animations with Motion,
        DVD:20–DVD:24
    content optimization with Compressor,
        DVD:15–DVD:20
    content optimization with QuickTime,
        DVD:12–DVD:15
    exporting chart animation for Final Cut
        Pro, DVD:29–DVD:32
    exporting images from Aperture,
        DVD:2–DVD:3
    layered Photoshop file for import,
        DVD:27–DVD:29
    motion backgrounds with LiveType,
        DVD:9–DVD:12
    PANTONE color strips in Photoshop,
        DVD:24–DVD:27
    text animations with LiveType,
        DVD:4–DVD:9
AIFF files, 64
album, creating in iPhoto, 50–51
animating presentations, 85–105
    builds for revealing text, 86–88
    Dashboard and, 103
    Exposé and, 103
    freeing up RAM, 99–100
    indexing with Spotlight, 98–99
    interleaved builds, 90–93
    mouse pointer behavior, 102–103
    overview, 85–86
    pausing/resuming slideshow, 106–107
    PowerPoint. *See* PowerPoint presentations
    preventing transitions from being
        clipped, 102
    running presentation, 104–106
    scaling slides up, 100–102
    sequence builds for revealing table, 88–90
    transitions between slides, 95–97
    troubleshooting, 107–109
    watching presentation, 93–94
animations. *See also* builds
    creating with Motion, DVD:20–DVD:24
    exporting chart animation for Final Cut
        Pro, DVD:29–DVD:32

motion backgrounds with LiveType, DVD:9–DVD:12
pie charts, 135–140
text animation with LiveType, DVD:4–DVD:9
title slides, 114–117
Aperture
exporting images, DVD:2–DVD:3
processing raw photo files, 317
Apple Authorized Training Centers, xvi
Apple Pro Training Series: Getting Started with Motion , DVD:22
Apple Pro Training Series: Motion , DVD:22
Apple Training Series, xvi
Arrange menu, 320
artwork. *See also* photos
adding to poster, 284–289
transparency added to, 180–186
audio
AAC files in iTunes, 66–67
adding to slideshows, 64
exporting GarageBand songs, 64–66
music bed added to slideshows, 67–69
podcast created with GarageBand, 224–229
system requirements, xv

B
B key, keyboard shortcut, 106
backgrounds
adding to brochures, 322–323
custom themes for, 161–164
motion backgrounds with LiveType, DVD:9–DVD:12
back-up files, 81–82
bar charts, animating, 132–135
basic text file (.txt), saving outlines in, 13
brochures, 309–333
background images, 322–323
building page one, 324–328

building page two, 328–333
importing photos, 319–322
overview, 309
preparing raw photo files for import, 316–319
template customization, 311–316
template selection, 310–311
Build Inspector, 16
builds
animating PowerPoint presentations. *See* PowerPoint presentations
Build Inspector, 16
interleaved, 90–93
revealing text, 86–88
sequence builds to reveal tables, 88–90
troubleshooting, 107
bullet points
cleaning up, 35–36
modifying, 21–23
styling, 32–33

C
C key, keyboard shortcut, 103
calculations, performing in tables, 40–42
capitalization, standard for video scripts, 338
card. *See* postcard
CD-ROM, exporting to, 200–201
cells, filling, 40–42
Chart Inspector, 16
charts, exporting animation for Final Cut Pro, DVD:29–DVD:32
charts, PowerPoint
animating, 127–128
bar charts, 132–135
cleaning up, 118–122
enhancing, 122–126
pie charts, 135–140
style, 140–145
Classic Brochure template, 310
clips, adding to movie, 72–74

colors
    charts, 125–126
    customizing in Pages, 256–258
    modifying, 24–25
    PANTONE color strips in Photoshop,
        DVD:24–DVD:27
    posters, 279–284
columns
    building brochure page one, 324–328
    building brochure page two, 328–333
    customizing for brochure, 314–316
commands
    for boldfacing text, 21
    for displaying Editor, 226
    for displaying Media Browser, 226
    for duplication, 277
    for opening font panel, 158
    for opening movie properties, 192
    point sizing, 245
    for quitting open applications, 100
    for saving, 81
    for selecting all, 29
    for switching between open applications,
        14
comments, adding, 148–150
compressed movies, scaling, 79
Compressor
    animated background files and, DVD:12
    optimizing content, DVD:15–DVD:20
content, video
    optimizing with Compressor,
        DVD:15–DVD:20
    optimizing in QuickTime,
        DVD:12–DVD:15
controls, playback, 94
copyright
    audio files and, 64
    shortcut for copyright symbol, 275
custom themes. *See* themes

D
Dashboard, 100–102
deletion, navigation shortcut, 105
disk space, system requirements, xv
Document Inspector, 16
documents. See also brochures; PowerPoint
    presentations; text
    one-sheet, 304–306
Down Arrow, navigation shortcut, 104–105
DVD drive, system requirements, xv
DVD, publishing presentation to, 217–223

E
Editor, displaying, 226
effects, build. *See* builds
empty themes, 156–157
equals sign (=)
    to navigate slide switcher, 105
    in table calculations, 40–41
Esc key, 80
exporting
    to CD-ROM, 200–201
    chart animation for Final Cut Pro,
        DVD:29–DVD:32
    to Flash, 215–216
    GarageBand song, 64–66
    to HTML, 223–224
    images, 214–215
    images from Aperture, DVD:2–DVD:3
    images to create podcast, 224–228
    to PDF, 212–214
    poster to PDF, 289–290
    to PowerPoint, 211–212
    to QuickTime, 208–211
Exposé, 103

F
F key, keyboard shortcut, 106

files
>   accessing media files, 48
>   audio formats, 64
>   back-up files, 81–82
>   Photoshop file compatibility with
>   Keynote, 180
>   preparing raw photo files for import,
>   316–319
Final Cut Pro, exporting chart animation for,
>   DVD:29–DVD:32
Flash, exporting to, 215–216
fonts. *See also* text
>   in brochures, 325
>   installing on presentation machine, 81
>   LiveFonts, DVD:6
>   opening Font panel, 158
formats. *See also* templates
>   audio files, 64, 66–67
>   image exports, 215
>   outlines saved in text format, 13
>   Photoshop files saved as, 170
>   QuickTime movies, 191–194
formulas, in table calculations, 40–42
forward slash (/), 106

G

GarageBand
>   creating podcast using, 224–229
>   exporting songs, 64–66
Graphic Inspector
>   adding drop shadow, 29–30
>   defined, 16
>   modifying shape object, 24–25
graphics
>   animations with Motion,
>   DVD:20–DVD:24
>   exporting to CD-ROM, 200–201
>   masking photos with shapes, 187–189
>   PowerPoint support for, 212

presentations in kiosk mode, 199–200
>   transparency added to artwork, 180–186
grouped objects, 288

H

H key, keyboard shortcut, 107
H.264 compressed movie, scaling, 79
handouts
>   creating storyboard handout, 347–350
>   printing, 206–207
>   printing multiple slides per page with
>   notes, 205
header row, 38–39
Help key, 106
HTML, exporting to, 223–224
Hyperlink Inspector, 16
hyperlinks
>   adding and navigating with, 194–199
>   embedding/formatting QuickTime
>   movies, 191–194
>   embedding Web pages, 189–191
>   exporting to CD-ROM, 200–201
>   in Pages documents, 331
>   running presentation in kiosk mode,
>   199–200
hyphenation, disabling, 278

I

iDVD, publishing presentation to, 217–223
iLife
>   adding media to presentation, 64
>   installing, xv
>   system requirements, xiv–xv
images. *See also* photos
>   background added to brochures, 322–323
>   editing image placeholders, 246–249
>   exporting, 214–215
>   exporting from Aperture, DVD:2–DVD:3
>   exporting to create podcast, 224–228
>   for market package project, 272–273

masks for cropping, 249–256
    sizing/flipping, 178
iMovie HD. *See* videos
indexing, with Spotlight, 98–99
Inspector windows, 16
interleaved builds, 90–93
Internet
    embedding Web pages, 189–191
    exporting presentation to HTML,
        223–224
    publishing to .mac, 345–347
iPhoto. *See* photos
iTunes. *See* audio
iWeb. *See* Web

J

J key, playback controls, 94

K

K key, playback controls, 94
keyboard shortcuts
    accessing, 106
    for duplicating postcards, 297–299
    for navigating, 104–105
    for pausing/resuming slideshows,
        106–107
    for playback controls, 94
    for quitting, 100
    for showing/hiding mouse pointer, 103
Keynote. *See also* advanced techniques;
    animating presentations; graphics;
    hyperlinks; media; publishing
    presentations; script/storyboard
    presentations; themes
    converting PowerPoint to. *See* PowerPoint
        presentations
    creating presentations. *See* presentations,
        creating
    launching, 4–5
kiosk mode, running presentations, 199–200

L

L key, playback controls, 94
laptop, giving presentation with, 229–232
layered Photoshop files, DVD:27–DVD:29
layout. *See also* templates
    adding more pages to newsletter layout,
        259–263
    completing newsletter layout, 264–268
    inserting pages in newsletter layout,
        263–264
    Masters button for choosing, 8
    presentation. *See* presentations, creating
    of storyboard proposal, 351–353
Left Arrow, navigation shortcut, 105
lesson files, installing from DVD, xv–xvi
LiveFonts, DVD:6
LiveType
    creating motion background with,
        DVD:9–DVD:12
    text animation with, DVD:4–DVD:9
Loren Ipsum, as placeholder text, 241

M

.mac, publishing presentation to, 345–347
Mac OS X
    prerequisites for getting started, xiii
    system requirements, xiv
marketing package, 271–307
    assembling project assets, 272–273
    one-sheet creation, 304–306
    overview, 271–272
    postcard back design, 299–304
    postcard front design, 292–294
    postcard, repeating, 297–299
    postcard template, 290–291
    postcard text, 294–297
    poster artwork, 284–289
    poster colors/sizes, 279–284
    poster placeholder text, 274–278

poster, saving for multiple purposes, 289–290

poster template, 273–274

masks

images, 249–256

photos, 61–63

shapes for masking photos, 187–189

master slide

building to create photo cutouts, 170–174

selecting, 7–8

media, 47–83

AAC files in iTunes, 66–67

accessing files, 48

albums in iPhoto, 50–51

audio added to slideshows, 64

clips added to movies, 72–74

exporting GarageBand song, 64–66

exporting to QuickTime, 208–211

music bed added to slideshow, 67–69

optimizing video for playback, 74–77

overview, 47

photo enhancement with iPhoto, 51–56

photo masks, 61–63

photo straightening, 60–61

photos added to iPhoto, 49–50

photos added to slides, 56–59

presentations with, 81–82

slide duplication, 80–81

still photos, 48

video added to slides, 77–80

video preparation in iMovie HD, 69–71

Media Browser, displaying, 226

memory. See RAM

Metrics Inspector

defined, 16

positioning photos, 59–61

scaling movies, 79–80

sizing/flipping images, 178

Microsoft PowerPoint. See PowerPoint

Microsoft Word, opening document, 145–146

minus sign (−), 106

motion background, DVD:9–DVD:12

Motion, creating animations, DVD:20–DVD:24

mouse pointer, changing, 102–103

movies. See videos

MP3 files, 64

music. See audio

N

narration. See audio

navigation

with hyperlinks, 194–199

navigator view, 17

shortcuts, 104–105

newsletters, 235–269

colors, customizing, 256–258

editing image placeholders, 246–249

exporting to PDF, 268–269

launching Pages, 236–237

layout, adding more pages, 259–263

layout, completing, 264–268

layout, inserting pages, 263–264

mask for cropping images, 249–256

overview, 235–236

replacing placeholder text, 241–246

templates, choosing, 237–239

templates, working with, 239–241

notes

adding/printing speaker notes, 204–206

adding to presentation, 148–150

printing as handouts, 206–207

O

one-sheet document, 304–306

Option key

for entering copyright symbol, 275

playing slideshow and, 94

using to duplicate postcard, 297–299

outline view
    adding slides, 11–12
    creating first slide, 10
    outlining presentation, 9–10
    pasting text into outline, 12–15

P

P key, navigation shortcut, 105
Page Down, navigation shortcut, 104–105
Page Up, navigation shortcut, 105
Pages. *See also* marketing package; newsletters
    color customization, 256–258
    hyperlinks/addresses in Pages documents, 331
    opening Word files, 145–146
    script/storyboard presentation. *See* script/storyboard presentations
    three-panel brochure. *See* brochures
PANTONE color strip, DVD:24–DVD:27
passwords, in kiosk mode, 199
PDF files
    controlling PDF file size, 214
    exporting newsletter to, 268–269
    exporting poster to, 289–290
    exporting to, 212–214
photos. *See also* images
    adding to iPhoto, 49–50
    adding to poster, 284–289
    adding to slides, 56–59
    album in iPhoto, 50–51
    cut-outs in custom themes, 164
    enhancing, 51–56
    exporting, 214–215
    exporting to create podcast, 224–228
    importing for brochure, 319–322
    masking, 61–63
    masking with shapes, 187–189
    raw files for import, 316–319
    still, 48
    straightening, 60–61

Photoshop
    compatibility with Keynote, 180
    PANTONE color strip, DVD:24–DVD:27
    photo cutouts, 165–170
    preparing layered file for import, DVD:27–DVD:29
    processing raw photo files, 317
pie charts, animating, 135–140
pixels, converting, 76
placeholders
    editing image in newsletter, 246–249
    replacing in poster, 274–278
    replacing text in newsletter, 241–246
playback
    controls, 94
    Exposé/Dashboard and, 103
    freeing up RAM, 99–100
    in kiosk mode, 199–200
    mouse pointer behavior and, 102–103
    preventing transitions from being clipped, 102
    scaling slides up, 100–102
    troubleshooting, 107–109
plus symbol (+)
    in formatting text in shapes, 27–28
    using to navigate slide switcher, 105
PNG format, saving Photoshop files, 170
podcast, creating using GarageBand, 224–229
point sizing, 245
pointer, mouse, 102–103
postcard
    adding text, 294–297
    designing back, 299–304
    designing front, 292–294
    repeating, 297–299
    template, 290–291
poster
    adding artwork, 284–289
    changing colors/sizes, 279–284

replacing placeholder text, 274–278

saving for multiple purposes, 289–290

template, 273–274

power users. *See* advanced techniques

PowerPoint, exporting to, 211–212

PowerPoint presentations, 111–153

    bar charts, 132–135

    chart animation, 127–128

    chart clean up, 118–122

    chart enhancement, 122–126

    chart style, 140–145

    comments added to, 148–150

    importing, 112–114

    overview, 111–112

    pie charts, 135–140

    rehearsing, 151–152

    slide content, 145–148

    table enhancement, 129–132

    title slides, 114–117

presentations. See animating presentations;
graphics; hyperlinks; PowerPoint
presentations; publishing presentations;
script/storyboard presentations; themes

presentations, creating, 3–45

    bullet points, modifying, 21–23

    Inspector window and, 16

    launching Keynote, 4–5

    master slide selection, 7–8

    media added to. *See* media

    outlining, 9–10

    overview, 3

    rounded rectangle added to, 33–34

    slides added to, 11–12

    slides, cleaning up, 34–36

    slides, creating first, 10

    slides, formatting text on, 16–20

    spelling errors, correcting, 43–44

    styling bullet points, 32–33

    styling titles, 30–32

    table cells, filling, 40–42

    table header rows, filling, 38–39

    tables added to, 36–38

    text, pasting into outline, 12–15

    text, placing inside shapes, 25–30

    text, shape for holding, 23–25

    theme selection, 5–7

    titles, modifying, 21

Presenter Display, 151–152

presets, storing, DVD:22

previewing, 207

printing

    handouts, 206–207

    speaker notes, 204–206

projector, hooking up to laptop, 229–232

proposals, laying out in Pages, 351–353

publishing presentations, 203–232

    adding/printing speaker notes, 204–206

    creating podcast using GarageBand,
        224–229

    exporting images, 214–215

    exporting to Flash, 215–216

    exporting to HTML, 223–224

    exporting to PDF, 212–214

    exporting to PowerPoint, 211–212

    exporting to QuickTime, 208–211

    giving presentation with laptop, 229–232

    to .mac, 345–347

    overview, 203

    printing handouts, 206–207

    sending to iDVD, 217–223

Q

Q key, 100

question mark (?), 106

QuickTime

    adding media to presentation, 47

    content optimization, DVD:12–DVD:15

    embedding/formatting movies, 191–194

exporting to, 208–211

H.264 compressed movie requirements, 79

Inspector, 16

Keynote audio file support, 64

Pro with animated background file, DVD:12

system requirements, xv

R

RAM

    freeing up, 99–100

    system requirements, xiv–xv

    VRAM requirements for smooth playback, 107–109

raw files

    exporting from Aperture, DVD:2–DVD:3

    preparing raw photo files for import, 316–319

rehearsing PowerPoint presentation, 151–152

remote controls, 232

resolution

    in Keynote themes, 7

    scaling slides up, 100–102

    troubleshooting, 107–109

resources, iWork, xvi–xvii

right bracket (]), navigation shortcut, 105

rows, header, 38–39

S

saving

    back-up files, 81–82

    custom themes, 174–175

    outlines in text format, 13

    Photoshop files, 170

    poster for multiple purposes, 289–290

script/storyboard presentations, 335–353

    creating, 340–345

    handout creation, 347–350

    laying out proposal, 351–353

    overview, 335–336

    publishing to .mac, 345–347

    saving template for video script, 336–339

searching with Spotlight, 98–99

sequence builds, 88–90

shapes

    adding rounded rectangle, 33–34

    adding to hold text, 23–25

    masking photos with, 187–189

    placing text inside, 25–30

Shift

    using to duplicate postcard, 297–299

    using to navigate slides, 105

sizes, changing in poster, 279–284

slides

    adding, 11–12

    cleaning up, 34–36

    creating first, 10

    duplicating, 80–81

    formatting text on, 16–20

    photos added to, 56–59

    replacing content, 145–148

    scaling up, 100–102

    selecting master slide, 7–8

    Slide Inspector, 16

    slide master for creating photo cutouts, 170–174

    title. *See* titles

    transitions between, 95–97

    troubleshooting poor play, 107–109

slideshows. *See also* animating presentations; presentations

    AAC files in iTunes, 66–67

    audio added to, 64

    clips added to movies, 72–74

    exporting GarageBand song for, 64–66

    music bed added to, 67–69

    optimizing video for playback, 74–77

    pausing/resuming, 106–107

preparing video in iMovie HD, 69–71

video added to slides, 77–80

spacebar, 106–107

speaker notes

adding/printing, 204–206

printing as handouts, 206–207

spelling errors, fixing, 43–44

Spotlight, indexing with, 98–99

stacking order, 320

storyboard presentations. *See* script/
storyboard presentations

styles

bullet, 32–33

chart, 140–145

shape, 33–34

text, 325

title, 30–32

symbols, for navigation, 197–198

system requirements, xiv–xv

T

Table Inspector, 16

tables

adding, 36–38

creating sequence builds to reveal, 88–90

filling cells, 40–42

filling header row, 38–39

PowerPoint, enhancing, 129–132

techniques, advanced. *See* advanced techniques

templates

brochures, 310–311

choosing for newsletters, 237–239

customizing for brochure, 311–316

HD templates for charts, DVD:32

postcards, 290–291

posters, 273–274

proposals saved as, 353

video scripts, 336–339

working with newsletter, 239–241

text

adding to postcard, 294–297

animating with LiveType, DVD:4–DVD:9

building brochure page one, 324–328

building brochure page two, 328–333

builds for revealing, 86–88

cleaning up, 34–35

in custom theme title page, 158–160

formatting in custom themes, 161–164

formatting on slide, 16–20

modifying in bullet points, 21–22

modifying in title, 21

pasting into outline, 12–15

placing inside shape, 25–30

replacing placeholder, 241–246

replacing placeholder in poster, 274–278

shapes for holding, 23–25

spelling errors, 43–44

Text Inspector, 16

themes

applying custom, 176–180

background/formatting text, 161–164

building Keynote slide master, 170–174

choosing, 5–7

empty, 156–157

exporting to CD-ROM, 200–201

overview, 155–156

photo cutouts, 164

preparing Photoshop file to create photo
cutout, 165–170

running presentation in kiosk mode,
199–200

saving/sharing, 174–175

title pages, 158–160

three-panel brochure. *See* brochures

TIFF format, converting raw photo files to,
316–319

titles

animating, 114–117

creating in custom themes, 158–160

ending with title slide, 80–81

modifying, 21

styling, 30–32

toolbar, displaying buttons, 285

transitions

adding to slideshow, 72–74

creating between slides, 95–97

preventing from being clipped, 102

troubleshooting, 107

transparency

adding to artwork, 180–186

creating animations with Motion, DVD:20–DVD:24

troubleshooting, animated presentation, 107–109

.txt (basic text file), saving outlines in, 13

U

Understanding Adobe Photoshop: Digital Imaging Concepts and Techniques, 156

Up Arrow, navigation shortcut, 105

V

videos

adding clips to movies, 72–74

adding to slides, 77–80

Compressor for optimizing content, DVD:15–DVD:20

duplicating slides, 80–81

exporting chart animation for Final Cut Pro, DVD:29–DVD:32

optimizing for playback, 74–77

preparing in iMovie HD, 69–71

QuickTime for optimizing content, DVD:12–DVD:15

templates for script, 336–339

views, navigator, to browse/modify, 17

views, outline. *See* outline view

VRAM, requirements for smooth playback, 107–109

W

W key, 107

Web

addresses in Pages documents, 331

embedding Web pages, 189–191

exporting presentation to HTML, 223–224

publishing to .mac, 345–347

windows

resizing, 285

working with Inspector, 16

Word document, opening, 145–146